HOW DO YOU DO BELONGING?

INSIGHTS FROM LEADERS FOR REFLECTION AND ACTION

HANNAH COSTANZO

hachette LEARNING

hachette LEARNING

Together we unlock every learner's unique potential

At Hachette Learning (formerly Hodder Education), there's one thing we're certain about. No two students learn the same way. That's why our approach to teaching begins by recognising the needs of individuals first.

Our mission is to allow every learner to fulfil their unique potential by empowering those who teach them. From our expert teaching and learning resources to our digital educational tools that make learning easier and more accessible for all, we provide solutions designed to maximise the impact of learning for every teacher, parent and student.

Aligned to our parent company, Hachette Livre, founded in 1826, we pride ourselves on being a learning solutions provider with a global footprint.

www.hachettelearning.com

To order, please visit www.HachetteLearning.com or contact Customer Service at education@hachette.co.uk / +44 (0)1235 827827.

ISBN: 978 1 0360 2059 0

First published in 2026 by
Hachette Learning (a trading division of Hodder & Stoughton Limited),
An Hachette UK Company
Carmelite House
50 Victoria Embankment
London EC4Y 0DZ

www.HachetteLearning.com

The authorised representative in the EEA is Hachette Ireland, 8 Castlecourt Centre, Dublin 15, D15 XTP3, Ireland (email: info@hbgi.ie)

Impression number 10 9 8 7 6 5 4 3 2 1
Year 2030 2029 2028 2027 2026

Illustrations by DC Graphic Design Limited, Hextable, Kent.
Typeset in the UK.
Printed in the UK.

A catalogue record for this title is available from the British Library.

FSC www.fsc.org MIX Paper | Supporting responsible forestry FSC™ C104740

About the author

Hannah Costanzo is Head of Policy at PiXL, the UK's largest education leadership network, where she works at the intersection of school improvement policy and everyday practice. Alongside school leaders Hannah looks to understand how the wider social and educational ecosystem shapes what happens in classrooms and corridors. Living and working in the northeast of England, she is aware of the regional disparities and inequities that affect the work that happens in schools and education settings – which is why she champions contextualised approaches over one-size-fits-all solutions.

In a context where many of the inequities that school leaders aim to address lie outside their direct sphere of influence, Hannah is passionate about understanding how school leaders create and retain their professional agency to act positively despite the very real challenges in society at large.

How do you do belonging? is her first book and the process of writing it has deepened her belief that there are school leaders across the country who are leading their institutions with strategic clarity and a lot of heart.

To all those working to turn hope into reality –
we see you and we're grateful.

Acknowledgements

The biggest and most important thanks must go to the leaders who have contributed their insights to this book: Matthew Stevens, David McPartlin, Lucy Burnett, Harvey Sarai, Jez Thomas, Chris Anders, Ella Capaldi, Stephen Mitchell, Miriam Riddell, Lucy Gowland, Elaine Johnston, Sarah Judge, Deneen Kenchington and Oli McVeigh. This is the first book I have written, and they have each been extraordinarily gracious and patient through the process. I am forever aware of the demands placed on school leaders' time, and I am incredibly grateful for every minute that they have been able to spare me. It's a real privilege to be able to celebrate their work.

I owe a debt of thanks to my leaders at PiXL – especially Rachel Johnson and Christina Moody – for giving me the opportunity to write this book. It has been the hardest and best thing I have done so far in my career. I am grateful to work for an organisation filled with brilliant, thoughtful, reflective people – many of whom have contributed (probably without realising it) to my thinking, and some of whom have offered direct and much-needed support, guidance and challenge throughout the process.

Thanks also due to the team at Hachette Learning who have been so helpful throughout this process.

If you'll forgive me for sounding trite – I'm also incredibly grateful to the wider education sector. Amidst some very real challenges, my professional network is a constant source of inspiration, possibility and hope. I have tried to write a book that contributes to that.

And finally, thank **you** for reading.

Contents

Foreword

For 25 years, PiXL has been a force for good in education, believing that stronger leaders create stronger schools. Working across 42,000 leaders, we have aimed to be principled, caring and brave together, and as a network we have shared the challenges and the opportunities in leading schools. Initially born out of the London Challenge, PiXL has always put collaboration and support at its heart believing that between us we know more than if we are alone.

There is no better exemplification of that work than this 'How do you do…' series. The aim of the series is to take nuanced themes, such as belonging, and to explore the various and diverse ways that school leaders are approaching them strategically and contextually. Underpinned by evidence and by the practical outworking in schools, each school leader has approached the challenge differently because their context is different.

We are not writing about silver-bullets in this series, we are exploring ideas together and recognising that not everything will work for everybody, and neither should it, that isn't the point. The point is that in understanding what others do and why, we are able to find the inspiration for our own context.

The school leaders in this book would be the first to admit they don't have all the answers, that there is work still to be done and that they will have to adapt as their contexts inevitably change. That is the case for all of us. But the important thing is that we start and we try. As you will discover in the book, belonging is not a fixed and final outcome – it requires maintenance and consistent care so that all those who are part of our community know they are valued and know they add value.

In a world where algorithms, bots and AI are promising connection and belonging but not always delivering on that promise, schools must be different. We must be different. We know the transformational difference knowledge through education makes, we know outcomes unlock doors, that knowledge creates opportunity. We have known this for decades. We also now know the difference belonging and mattering make on the future life chances and outcomes of young people. It is not outcomes OR life chances, it is both/and. It is not knowledge over belonging, it is both.

When we do both, we not only have young people who can excel with the knowledge they have learned, they can also thrive in the belief that they matter. Both of these things will last for the rest of their lives, long before they leave us.

That is the remarkable thing about the work of schools: we are not playing the finite game, but an infinite one. All the measurements may be at the end of key stages, but the impact lasts a lifetime.

I hope this 'How do you do…' series helps bring clarity to your thinking around themes that can be hard to pin down in practice, so that you can be clear about what the right next steps are for you. That is certainly the intention. And when you take an idea, adapt it for your context and see impact, then share it. Together, we create stronger leaders, stronger schools, stronger futures.

Rachel Johnson, Series Editor and CEO of PiXL

Introduction

We do not need to look far to find evidence of not-belonging in the world today: from political polarisation and social fragmentation to loneliness emerging as a major public health concern. And so it is not surprising perhaps that we are seeing increasing evidence of this (to greater or lesser extents) within our schools: whether it be rising persistent absence, ongoing teacher retention challenges or a breakdown in the social contract between parents and school.

If that's what an absence of belonging looks like, what does true belonging look like in an educational setting? As you'll discover as you read this book, there is room for each setting to interpret and codify exactly what they mean by belonging – but a helpful starting point might be that belonging is the experience of feeling that you matter to a community, and that it matters to you.

We have known for some time that a strong sense of belonging in schools can impact positively on children and young people's achievement, attendance and wellbeing (examples of recent reports and research include Greany *et al.*, 2023; Riley, Coates and Allen, 2020; Robinson, Culbert and Smith, 2025). We also know that the impact is long term, with those reporting a sense of belonging in childhood and adolescence being more likely to exhibit positive psychological functioning across a range of variables into later adulthood (Allen, 2020).

A strong sense of belonging in schools should also help us safeguard children and young people against the pernicious and divisive narratives being pedalled by bad actors on social media who seek to profit from young people's insecurities and anxieties. As Allen states in *The Psychology of Belonging* (2020): 'Research into school shootings, radicalisation, mental illness, chronic loneliness, social isolation and suicide have one thing in common: an inverse relationship with belonging. Examining our need to belong has never been more important as we strive to tackle some of the most complex social issues of our time.'

And that is all the time I am going to spend on **why** belonging is important, because at this point I am going to take it as read that you believe that, given that you are reading this book. (You can, however, find plenty of references at the end of this book if you want to explore further.)

Because this book is not about why, it's about **how** we build belonging.

If we are going to explore how we can actively build cultures of belonging in our schools and settings, we need to address two things.

1. Belonging as a positive approach

I have outlined some of the negative consequences that can emerge from a lack of belonging, and it is perhaps natural that we may want to act defensively to avoid not-belonging. But trying to stop something bad happening is not as empowering as trying to **make something good happen**. We deserve a positive approach.

2. Belonging as a practice

Belonging can be understood as a product, but it can be more helpful to think of it as a **practice**. By focusing on the actions that we take to consciously build a sense of belonging within our schools, we can focus on what we are able to influence. It helps us control the controllables.

So this book aims to do these two things.

- Share practice and insights with you from a wide variety of settings (how **others** do belonging).
- Help you recognise and articulate what you are doing to cultivate a sense of belonging in your own setting (how **you** do belonging).

How others do belonging: Sharing practice

I am privileged to be able to share insights from ten different schools, with each chapter focusing on a different school. While the big picture 'why' is often similar across schools, the nuances in needs, contexts and settings means that the individual practice and mechanisms for belonging will necessarily look different in each setting. What we have tried to do with this book is to draw out both the **thinking** and the **practice**, to hopefully provide leaders with plenty of food for thought and action.

There is a brief one-sentence overview of some of the key areas of focus and approach explored in each chapter below as well as the type of school, which may be useful for prioritising your reading (although I would caution against skipping chapters from different sectors as there is so much to be gained from reflecting across the different stages of education).

Saracens High School, London: A free school that builds belonging through a deliberate and supportive family culture, and values of hard work, discipline, humility and honesty (shared with their parent organisation, Saracens Rugby Club) that promote individual agency and responsibility.

Flakefleet Primary School, Lancashire: An outward-looking and deeply relational school that positions itself as the beating heart of its community, nurturing belonging through unconditional belief in every child.

Bantock Primary School, Wolverhampton: A highly mobile and diverse primary school that leads with curiosity, building belonging through careful listening and an ambitious culture of inclusion.

Park Community School, Hampshire: A school that seeks to dismantle the boundary between school and community, using physical space and enterprise to make belonging tangible.

King's Cross Academy, London: A primary school navigating a striking tension between its affluent surroundings and the real lives of its families, building belonging by helping children feel they belong not just in school but in the wider world on their doorstep.

Deeside Sixth Form, Flintshire: A sixth form college that leans into students' desire for a fresh start, building belonging by creating a culture that is intentionally distinct from school and that prioritises trust, authenticity and the freedom to show up as yourself.

Acklam Grange School, Middlesbrough: A large 11–16 academy that counters negative narratives about place and identity, by building belonging through civic pride and an inclusive school culture.

Harmony Primary School, Belfast: A primary school where belonging is built on togetherness, restorative practice and deep family partnership.

Richard Barnes Academy, Peterborough: An alternative provision seeking to repair the relationship their students have with education through structure, care and therapeutic practice.

Ferndown Upper School, Dorset: A co-educational school in a highly selective area that challenged itself to understand why school wasn't working for its boys, and in doing so strengthened belonging for the whole community.

Concepts like belonging can feel intangible and difficult to articulate, and so to anchor us on this journey we have borrowed from Kathryn Riley's excellent research into belonging in schools (Riley, Coates and Perez Martinez, 2018). She concludes that when belonging is placed at the heart of a school, there are three key things at play.

- **Space and place**: The way that physical places and emotional spaces have a profound impact on our sense of self and sense of place.
- **Relations**: The quality of the relationships and the extent to which we feel known and seen for who we truly are.
- **Agency**: How able or well-equipped we feel to 'intervene in the world' and make valuable contributions.

So, you will see in each chapter that we have used these headings, with every school exploring how their practice aligns with each of these areas. This consistency to the chapters should enable you to make parallels and connections between practice across different settings - and your own, of course!

How you do belonging: Reflecting on your own practice

I have two things that I want to make absolutely clear at this point.

- I am not suggesting that you ought to be doing everything featured in this book. It is not a to-do list.
- I am also not suggesting that you are not **already doing** some of the practice in this book.

Every school is different and will be on its own unique journey with belonging.

Now that is clear, I do want to ensure that you have regular and varied opportunities to reflect on your own practice as you read this book. To that end, at the close of each chapter you will find some **reflective questions**. They are split into two themes: reflecting on your current practice, and considering future action. Depending on where you are in your own journey, you may choose to focus on one set of questions, or both, or ignore them all entirely - whatever is most helpful. You may find it useful to have a pen and paper, or some more technologically-advanced form of note-taking, to hand as you read.

In addition, there are four **time to think** interludes that break up the chapters and aim to provide you with some additional research, theory or frameworks for reflecting on different aspects of belonging. Again, use these to the extent that they are helpful for you.

Regardless of where you are in your career, and where your setting is on the journey of cultivating belonging, I hope this book is a useful tool for providing insight, generating new ideas, challenging your thinking and affirming your own practice.

Saracens High School, London

Dr Matthew Stevens, Principal

About us and our community

At Saracens High School, we take our values of discipline, hard work, honesty and humility from our parent organisation, Saracens Rugby Club, and like the club, 'we exist to have a positive impact on as many people as possible.' The values are central to our culture and run through everything we do, for adults as well as the young people.

Saracens is a free school in Barnet, North London, which opened in 2018 with a cohort of 157 Year 7 students. Seven years later, we are a thriving community of 1200, including 280 students in our sixth form. We serve a densely populated and wonderfully diverse community with very high levels of deprivation, in an area with no other mixed comprehensive schools within a 40-minute bus ride. We typically have around 75 different ethnicities represented and over 50 different languages spoken by our school community, with well over 50% of our young people being eligible for free school meals.

What belonging means to us

Generating a sense of belonging is the essential ingredient required to unite diverse groups of people into a cohesive community. It starts with culture and ethos, which is nurtured by all the adults, and infiltrates all we do, from curriculum design to recruitment to everyday interactions.

For us, the true measure of our success is in the lives that the young people we serve go on to lead, and 'who they are', not grades, outcomes or awards. (We are not discounting these completely, they just aren't as important as the young people themselves.) We know that most young people throughout the country have more advantages than the majority of our children, and so we work hard to remove barriers and provide opportunities and experiences to level the playing field.

Saracens High School is a place that focuses on the development of our values and generating a family ethos. The values originated from thinking about the attributes that all successful people have in any walk of life: they are disciplined, they work hard and they are honest – with themselves and with others. When the Rugby Club started achieving success, they added the fourth and final value: humility. These values are brought to life every day by our students and staff: discipline and hard work in the classroom, honesty and humility in the way we conduct ourselves.

We had the advantage of starting our journey as a school with just Year 7 – when all members of staff knew every pupil and it genuinely felt like a large family. We knew that would not last as our community grew, and so we put strategies in place such as family lunch, smaller learning groups and family read. These strategies ensure that as we grow, we are able to maintain our close connections, where every pupil feels known, valued and heard.

Relations

All schools strive to build community and relationships, and so many of the strategies we have at Saracens, such as a thriving House system with regular competitions, will be very familiar. Below are some of the things that we do that might not be so commonplace and have most positively impacted on the quality of relationships at Saracens.

Learning Groups and Learning Coaches

We know that when students transition from primary school into much larger secondary schools, they can feel a little lost and anonymous. Like many schools, pupils are assigned a House when they join us in Year 7. However, we also then split this group into two to give a ratio of one member of staff to 15 pupils. This is their Learning Group and the staff member responsible for their group is their Learning Coach.

The aim is for our Learning Coaches to develop strong relationships with every one of the children in their Learning Group, including getting to know their wider families.

- Pupils are in their Learning Groups for 30 minutes each morning, and 30 minutes each afternoon (Monday–Thursday). During this time, they take part in family reading, contribute to the character passport, work on retrieval strategies and celebrate successes.
- Learning Coaches contact our families in the first few weeks of a new term, and every child will have a one-to-one check-in every few weeks.
- Learning Coaches are not just teaching staff; learning support assistants and cover supervisors are also part of the teams. With many of our LSAs and cover supervisors wanting to become teachers, this is an important part of their development, and we recognise the additional responsibilities financially.

We find this approach allows for really deep relationships to form and also ensures that staff have the capacity to be anticipatory and proactive (seeing pupils at the end of the day also provides an opportunity to resolve any issues that might have come up before they go home).

Family read

This is our read-aloud strategy that forms part of the Learning Group time across Years 7–11, typically two or three times a week. The aim of family read is to create time for reading for pleasure, giving accurate guidance and scaffolding, with novels that are carefully chosen with pleasure, transformation and inclusion in mind.

Each session is 30 minutes and during this time the adults in the room read fluently to the children, who follow along in their copy of the book. Since the adults take care of the difficult task of reading and decoding, pupils can focus completely on comprehension, critical thinking and engaging with the ideas in the stories. All pupils will read up to six complex texts per year, which include titles such as *Illegal* by Eoin Colfer and Andrew Donkin (Year 7), *Ground Zero* by Alan Gratz (Year 8) and *I Must Betray You* by Ruta Sepetys (Year 10).

Family lunch

We know that many of our families are single-parent families, and often the adult will be juggling commitments while trying to be the best parent they can be. We also know that research consistently demonstrates that a strong family unit will impact on the development of a young person, and one of the most powerful activities for building a strong family unit is to eat meals together as part of a regular routine. These investigations have shown that when children eat together frequently, they are more likely to have higher self-esteem, eat better diets and have stronger academic performance (Harrison *et al.*, 2015). Conversely, they are less likely to encounter serious challenges in later life through better risk mitigation and more social behaviours (Harrison *et al.*, 2015). Reflecting on this research, and what we know about the lived experiences of our pupils, we wanted to think differently about how we eat together at school.

Family lunch is a daily activity at Saracens that allows all pupils to eat a free, hot and nutritious meal each day. Across two sittings of 25 minutes each, our amazing catering team feed over 900 children. Food is served family-style, with all pupils eating the same meal. What's important to us, is **how** this happens.

Children belong to a lunch group of seven, who sit together every day at a round table. Year 7 pupils are allocated their seats during the first term, to help them get to know peers in their classes, but after that pupils can choose their groups.

Everyone at the table has a job.

- The **first** person collects a tray with the plates and cutlery and they lay the table.
- The **second** person collects the food from the serving hatch and serves the food to their friends (we quickly worked out that having them serve themselves last meant more equal portions for the group!).
- Once they have eaten together, the **third** pupil clears the dirty plates and trays to the side, at clearing stations that are usually manned by parents.
- The **fourth** pupil collects the dessert, and the **fifth** will take the used tray to the cleaning station.
- The final job, for the **sixth** and **seventh** pupils, is to clean the table and prepare for the next sitting (if they're in the first sitting), or to help the cleaners at the end by stacking the chairs.

With around eight members of staff in the hall, it is a time that reinforces self-regulation and collaboration, and, while I have never been brave enough to try it, I am convinced that pupils could run the lunch with no adult supervision.

Values-centred recruitment and induction

We are at our most effective when we work in an organisation that shares our values, so it's essential that our recruitment identifies those who will thrive in an environment like ours, and that our induction helps them feel part of the family from the outset.

Recruitment

For some positions, we long-list and conduct a seven-minute, two-question online interview to help us get to know the person and their values better. The questions are usually 'What are the key opportunities and key constraints that you have experienced in your life so far?' and 'Tell us three things that you will never compromise on.' It is surprising how much you can learn about a person from these questions.

Induction

Although similar in many ways, every school has their own unique processes, terminologies and contexts, and so the induction of new staff is an important part of the recruitment process. We try to be mindful that there is a lot of information to take in when we start a new school and you cannot memorise everything for the first week.

We run induction sessions on a Monday afternoon for staff who are new to the school. These take place in the autumn term. We buddy staff with an existing colleague, and SLT are each assigned new staff to check in with every couple of weeks. Through these first few weeks and months especially, we reinforce that we expect mistakes to be made and that there are no silly questions – and we always encourage the sharing of new ideas.

Agency

We have a responsibility to prepare young people for work and to foster a desire to make a positive contribution to society. We must help them to live our values, and to see life beyond childhood and beyond where they live, providing them with the information and support that will help them make dreams a reality. We want our young people to feel a sense of control over their direction in life.

Being future-focused

There is no shortage of aspiration from pupils nor their families, although they can often be limited to well-known, high-profile roles such as doctor or lawyer. Most of our pupils will not know anyone in those professions and do not know what it takes to be successful in those fields. We need both to help our pupils understand what these careers look like and how to be successful in them and to introduce them to a wide range of professions and vocations of which they may be unaware.

At Saracens, being future focused means helping students discover what sparks their interest and then preparing them for their next steps by helping them plan and equipping them with the skills and knowledge they need to be successful.

Discovery

Like most schools, we have a growing programme that helps pupils discover what careers are out there, including external speakers, visits and work placements. We host an annual My Future, My Choice event that brings over seventy professionals from a wide variety of backgrounds to our school. As the name suggests, the emphasis is always placed on **their choice**: if our pupils want to be doctors then that's brilliant and we'll support them to achieve that, but we want it to be their genuine choice. One of our sixth form students recently told a visitor to the school: 'A lot of people find their identity within Saracens'. That's what we want for all our pupils.

Choice is also important when pupils are considering their next steps after sixth form. Many of our young people will leave us to go to university or take up a degree apprenticeship: from our first key stage 5 cohort, 90% of students went to university (92% of our students eligible for free school meals) and 15% of our students secured places at Russell Group universities. But there are also many others who will look for work or a lower-level apprenticeship. We want to support each pathway equally, so we are proud of our one-year Pre-Apprenticeship programme in Year 12, which aims to prepare the students to be exceptional employees and gives them substantial work experience. When it works best, the young person will leave us to start work with their placement company.

Preparation

Preparation for life after school permeates many aspects of how the school operates.

- We know that if someone **lives the values** of discipline, hard work, honesty and humility they will be successful, and these are reinforced in lessons and conversations at every opportunity. One student recently wrote a thank you letter to the school upon gaining a place at university, in which she said: 'I will live these values for the rest of my life.'

- We **promote self-regulation**, for example through the family lunches and movement around the school (no silent corridors here, because that is not what happens at work!).
- We have **lead greeters** in every class. We get a lot of visitors to Saracens (especially because of our links with the rugby club) and our pupil lead greeters are responsible for approaching visitors to lessons, explaining what learning is taking place, sharing their work and making them feel welcomed to the class. We rotate lead greeters regularly, so at some point every pupil will have this responsibility. It's not only nice for the visitors to feel that they aren't interrupting, but it also clearly signals pupil ownership and agency over the learning that happens in our classes.
- We adopt many of Paul Dix's approaches to discipline with **three simple expectations**: be ready, be respectful, be safe.
- We have **reparation meetings** at break and after school instead of detentions, since very few employers adopt such a punitive approach.

Looking specifically at the sixth form, we have seminar groups, instead of forms, to help the students transition into their next step. There is a lot of exposure to university life and work through our external links, and a strong emphasis on preparing students for applications and interviews. Our support continues beyond Year 13, as regular contact with our alumni group maintains the link with the school and students know that they can contact us if they have any questions or are experiencing difficulties. Being part of the Saracens family doesn't stop when you leave.

Broadening horizons

As part of our commitment to helping pupils discover what inspires them, we have a strong focus at Saracens on providing multiple and varied opportunities to broaden pupils' horizons.

- In key stage 3, pupils undertake challenges in and outside of school to achieve **character passports** (bronze, silver and gold). The aim is not only to help pupils be 'GCSE-ready' but also 'Duke of Edinburgh-ready'. We are proud to offer the Duke of Edinburgh Bronze, Silver and Gold awards, and the take-up is high. Finance can often be a barrier to pupils taking part in DofE, so we subsidise this for pupils eligible for pupil premium funding, and we provide as much equipment as we can.

- We know there is a shortfall in exposure to arts subjects when pupils take their KS4 options, and we believe that it is important that all pupils still experience the arts in the older year groups. Every year, we run an **arts week**, which includes all pupils and staff in the school.
- Our programme of whole-school **Making Memories Days** ensures that all our pupils gain experiences that some might not otherwise have. These include experiences outside of school – a day at the beach, cinema trips, ice skating, scavenger hunts across London – as well as special days in school, including a market trading day, a circus skills day and a charity fundraising day. There are four days each year and these are funded largely by the school (a recent request for voluntary contributions from our families generated £900 from 1200 families).
- Our irrationally optimistic goal is for all pupils to take part in an **international visit** at some point in their time in school. We support those pupils who are eligible for the pupil premium grant to attend international visits as much as possible, but finance is a barrier we are yet to completely remove. However, the ambition remains and we will continue to provide opportunities that include visits to Berlin, Spain, ski trips and taking part in the World Challenge.

Leveraging our relationship with Saracens Rugby Club

We often have wonderful opportunities presented by our link with Saracens, either with the club directly or through their partner businesses and sponsors. Generally, the business liaisons have never worked in a school and often the logistical challenges are underestimated and the timelines are short. But the opportunities are immense, and so our default response is 'Yes!' and we work quickly and flexibly to remove any barriers in the way.

Our 'Yes' approach has led to pupils designing the kit for a high-profile game, appearing in advertising campaigns, accessing work placements and mentoring (for sixth form students), and even a last-minute visit from the Secretary of State for Culture and Sport.

Staff agency

Our culture of saying 'Yes!' extends to embracing staff ideas (although the yes is sometimes followed by an 'and' or a 'but'...). If someone has a passion and wants to give pupils an opportunity that they would not otherwise have, then we have a responsibility to try to make it happen.

So, when a member of staff recently asked, 'Can I organise a visit to Tanzania?' the answer was 'Yes, and what do we have to do to make that happen?' Our My Future, My Choice careers event is another outcome of our 'Yes!' policy.

It's also not just about ideas for the pupils. It has led also to changes to CPD that allow any member of staff, including ECTs, to lead and contribute to INSET sessions, as well as moving timetabled subject meetings to within the school day.

We take our lead from Will Guidara's *Unreasonable Hospitality* (2022): all ideas are welcomed, credited and celebrated, which builds the sense of belonging across the staff team.

Space and place

For us at Saracens, attending to the physical environment of the school has focused on creating unity and togetherness – whether that is in leveraging the brand through our association with the rugby club to reinforce our shared values and identity, or ensuring that the school is outward-facing and at the service of our community.

Branding

Branding has a strong link to belonging, and being a part of an organisation with an established brand is something that helped us to develop that sense of belonging from day one. The Saracens club colours of red and black run throughout the school and the uniform and serve as a visual reminder: this is our family, and you are part of something special.

Year 7 pupils are presented with their ties in their first assembly. The presentation is made by players from the men's and women's teams and other representatives from the wider Saracens organisation. The ties feature both the school badge and a stripe of colour representing their House.

The profile of the club in the community, and across London, means that we are often spotted when on educational visits and it's lovely to receive emails from members of the public praising pupils and staff on their conduct. Being recognised as part of the school, even when they are away from it, really helps to emphasise that belonging.

School facilities

Our vision speaks of the building being a hub for the local community. We regularly hire out our building and facilities – including our off-site AstroTurf pitch – at a reduced rate for local organisations that serve our community, such as tuition services, church groups and sports teams.

We have hosted the Citizen's Advice Bureau, using a meeting room by reception to make it more accessible to the community, and we are exploring the NHS using some of our site to run preventative clinics. They feel that members of the community are more likely to seek support at school, rather than going to a GP or hospital, and we are happy to support where we can.

Space to come together

Although our site is small for 1200 young people, we are blessed to have a new building, completed in 2021, and we were able to have some input into its design. A sense of family and community is at our core, and we are grateful to the Department for Education who heard our plea for a partition wall that opens up the assembly and dining spaces to be able to accommodate all of the young people at the same time. This is what allows us to accommodate family lunch every day, as well as our whole-school end of term assemblies (it's quite tight, but we can do it!).

Because our school is relatively new and grew slowly over time, we wanted to celebrate our first year of being a full school. To do this, we had a whole-school photograph taken at the Saracens stadium. This was a way of demonstrating to the children and staff that they are part of something bigger, and that their community – both local and the wider Saracens network and fans – supports them.

Lessons we have learned

- **Anything is possible**. There may be an impact somewhere else across the school, but being brave, flexible and knowing that the answer is somewhere in the building can lead to remarkable outcomes.
- **Values help forge identity**, and therefore a sense of belonging.
- The moment you lose the **intensity and frequency in reinforcing your uniqueness** is the moment staff and pupils will begin to think it is less important.

Time to think

<table>
<tr><th>Questions for reflecting on your current setting</th><th>Questions to consider for further action</th></tr>
<tr><td>
<ul>
<li>Often values are about the type of people we want to be and help our students to be. What impact does your setting's values have on what belonging feels like there? Try to be as specific as possible when writing your answers.</li>
<li>How do you communicate your values to staff and students joining your school? How do you seek to understand their values?</li>
<li>What aspects of your setting make it unique? How regularly and emphatically is this reinforced to your staff, students and wider community?</li>
</ul>
</td><td>
<ul>
<li>Bring to mind a recent suggestion or opportunity that was put to you by a member of your school community, that you chose not to say yes to. What were the reasons for saying no? What would have happened if you had said 'yes, and...' or 'yes, but...' instead?</li>
<li>What is your 'irrationally optimistic' goal for your school in terms of generating a sense of belonging for all? What makes it feel irrational? Or, to take the alternative perspective, what needs to change for it to feel rational?</li>
<li>'Being part of the Saracens family doesn't stop when you leave.' Where are the opportunities in your setting to ensure there is a legacy of belonging that remains even after students move on?</li>
</ul>
</td></tr>
<tr><td colspan="2">Your commitment for further reflection and action
1.
2.
3.</td></tr>
</table>

Flakefleet Primary School, Lancashire

David McPartlin, Headteacher

Lucy Burnett, Deputy Headteacher

About us and our community

At Flakefleet, building strong relationships and fostering a sense of belonging is at the heart of our work. We place a great emphasis on helping our children to believe in themselves, to take risks and to dare to dream. We like to think of ourselves as a happy, caring and innovative school that develops independent and resilient children.

We are a larger-than-average primary school based in Fleetwood, Lancashire, about seven miles north of Blackpool on the north-west coast of England. As with many coastal towns, there has been persistent economic decline over the last fifty years. The average household income in our area falls well below the average for England and Wales (according to National Office of Statistics data), and we see a lot of issues associated with this in our community including limited job opportunities, high crime rates and mistrust of schools, police and social care.

What belonging means to us

For us, belonging starts with our relationship to our community. We believe that if the school truly feels like it belongs to the community, then that will help individuals feel like they belong at our school. So we focus on ensuring that our school, and its approach, is harmonious with and responsive to the needs of the community we serve. Because of our socioeconomic context (and not in spite of it), we take an outward-facing stance, with much of our work centred on building strong bridges between the school and the community. We want our school to fit seamlessly into Fleetwood.

On an individual level, we aim for all staff and students at Flakefleet to feel empowered to be the change they want to see in the world and the community. Our school motto is #daretodream, and we are emphatic in our support for, and belief in, our children. We strive to ensure they feel understood and loved for their unique qualities, and this is underpinned by our relational approach. We appreciated these comments in our latest Ofsted inspection (May 2024): 'Flakefleet is a very special school. Pupils flourish. This is due to the loving support that they receive from the staff, who know them exceedingly well. This school truly sits at the heart of its community.' That's what belonging means to us.

Relations

We believe that strong relationships, grounded in kindness and respect, will lead to the best outcomes for our children. We embrace the importance of high support and high challenge in our relationships with staff, students and families, which we think leads to a culture that values trust and honesty.

Relational approach

We take a relational approach at Flakefleet, which for us means that our staff and students understand that a productive learning environment is achieved through exemplary behaviour and strong relationships. This is codified in our relational policy, which makes clear our expectations and guides staff to teach self-discipline over compliance (our relational policy has replaced what was once our behaviour policy). Through this we aim to build self-efficacy so that our children develop resilience and independence.

Much of the work of Paul Dix has informed our approach, which has a heavy emphasis on respectful behaviour for all and a restorative approach to managing poor conduct through emotion coaching.

Strategies that emphasise the positive

Our outlook on behaviour is positive, with all staff seeking to first pay attention to best conduct and to model the positive behaviours we want to see in school. We have a few positive strategies that we find work well with our students.

- A **recognition board** encourages social and learning behaviours. Children's names are moved onto the board when they have exhibited the target behaviour for the day. The aim is always that the whole class get on the board. Adults or pupils can nominate pupils and there is an emphasis on children working together as a team to get everyone on the board. Once a name is on the board, it cannot be removed.
- A **jar of joy** is displayed, either pictorially or physically, in each class. Each time the class work as a team to exhibit desired learning behaviour, a marble is placed in the jar. When the jar is full (no more than twice a half term), the class get 10 minutes of extra playtime.
- We use **postcards** for high-level recognition of an individual going over and above. It can be given to and from any member of the school community, whether child or adult, and whether staff member or visitor. There is no set amount each week and it must be sincere to keep its value. Postcards are written and posted into the post box, which SLT will then read before posting to the recipient's home address.

When things go wrong

When a child is not meeting our expectations for behaviour and we have to intervene, we have a clear set of steps that we follow. Our goal is always to de-escalate and decelerate any unwanted behaviours as quickly as possible. Staff will deal with the behaviour without delegating. For all of the steps outlined below, we try to manage behaviour privately where possible, which we believe helps build trust and demonstrates our respect for the children.

1. **Reminder**: Remind the child of our expectations: that they be safe, kind and ready. We repeat reminders where necessary, so children have the opportunity to self-correct.
2. **Advice**: Outline the behaviour that is failing to meet expectations and what needs to be done to fix it.
3. **30-second intervention**: Speak to the learner and give a final opportunity to engage through delivering a 30-second intervention script. We use a gentle approach that is personal and non-threatening, making sure we are at eye level or lower and to the side of the learner. The script highlights again the expectation, where it is not being met, and includes a reminder of when the child has previously exhibited the desired behaviour. The child is thanked for listening and given time to reflect.

4. **Emotion coaching**: If a child has had time out of their class, we have an emotion coaching conversation with them. This guides them to recognise their emotions as being natural, validates their feelings and helps them label and link emotions, as well as giving them an opportunity to problem-solve.

We find that this approach has really strengthened our relationships with the children at Flakefleet and also contributes to a calm and productive learning environment.

Putting the right support in place

We try to always be responsive to the needs of our community and are often adapting our provision in light of this.

SEN/SERF Unit

In September 2024, we opened a new key stage 1 SEN unit and an EYFS and key stage 1 SERF unit (Special Education Resource Facility). These are designed to provide specialised support for 16 children across Lancashire. They are dedicated spaces where each child receives personalised attention, supported by a high ratio of adults to children to ensure every child's unique needs are met. The unit is for pupils with communication and interaction difficulties.

The Little Lighthouse

This is our nursery provision for two-year-olds, which has really supported transition into full-time school for some children. Children enjoy continuous provision both indoors and outdoors. One of the drivers behind this was that we wanted to help non-working parents return to work earlier (if they wanted to) and to support low-income parents to remain in work.

Dedicated family worker

As part of our pastoral team, we have a dedicated family support worker who is on hand to lend a supportive ear and work individually with parents when needed. Parents are strongly encouraged to reach out if they are struggling, and we do what we can to support.

Magic Breakfast

At Flakefleet, we believe no child should ever be too hungry to learn. We are supported by the registered charity Magic Breakfast to feed children and to help end child morning hunger for good. Magic Breakfast is available every day for all children from Reception to Year 6.

Opening the doors to the community

From our perspective, a school that works cohesively with the community it serves is going to get the best results for its children. We've worked a lot over the last few years on how we do this.

We are represented on the regeneration board for the town, and that means we are able to situate the conversations we're having in school within the wider work happening in the area. We've been able to foster productive working relationships with our local police force, which has been particularly helpful in supporting some of our most vulnerable students.

We try to draw on these links whenever we're arranging events such as fairs and celebrations, and it really enriches the experience for us and for our children. We try to set the bar really high in terms of these events to keep them interesting and exciting for all our community members – in the summer of 2025 we had our Flakefleet Festival, featuring Whigfield as a musical act!

Space and place

We try to think carefully about the physical spaces in our school, so that we can maximise their utility and accessibility.

The Strive Café

Through the multi-agency relationships developed in our community, we were able to secure investment to build the Strive Café on our site, which was formerly a children's centre. This is a fully-staffed public café on our school site, which has become a real hub in our community. It is used not only by our students and their families, but also by our school staff and members of the wider community – from our local NHS workers to a regular group of retirees attending after their Wednesday aquafit classes. To help maintain our close links with the police force, we offer daily hot drinks to our local community police officers.

The café is an extension of the school, with plans in place for community volunteers to run it throughout the summer holidays (albeit with reduced hours) with organised activities several times a week. The hope is that this will help to maintain our relationships with the community over the summer. It also symbolises our investment and belief in our community

– we believe what we can make together can compete with the big brand chains.

The physical environment

We try to ensure that the school environment is calm and cared for, with low-arousal learning spaces to reduce over-stimulation. We make an effort, where possible, for the physical space to be warm and welcoming – we have a local artist who draws a seasonal montage on the windows at the main school entrance.

For spaces where we often meet with parents, we were inspired by the Danish principle of *hygge*: to create a cosy and warm atmosphere. We know that meetings in schools can often be anxiety inducing for parents, and we want them to feel as comfortable as possible. Our leadership office, where parents will often be if they're meeting with a member of SLT, has comfy sofas, deep warm painted walls and fairy lights – we want it to feel less like a school and more like a living room.

Use of space

We are really lucky at Flakefleet in that we have a large site and quite a lot of space, but we still try to use that space as effectively and efficiently as possible.

Over the years, we have identified a few rooms that were being used minimally throughout the day. Sometimes these were rooms that were used predominantly for storage, or were offices used by teaching staff who only spent an hour or two in them throughout the day.

We wanted to capitalise on the space we had, so that these spaces were being used for the maximum benefit of the whole school community. We brought people together into shared offices (Lucy and Dave now share an office), and in doing so were able to free up rooms to be used by the children throughout the day.

- The **Nurture Room** is a retreat away from the hustle and bustle of the school. It's the largest of these spaces, with sofas, a carpet area with beanbags and an activity area. Children spend supervised time here when they need a break from the busyness of the rest of the school.
- The **Zen Den** is the perfect place for children to come to when they are dysregulated or need to have a nap. It's a small room, with bean bags, plants and soft lighting.

- The **Quiet Room** is used when children need to work somewhere quieter and freer from discussion. It's set up more like a classroom, but with some softer lighting, and is most often used to keep learning going while children take a break from a class before returning to their peers.
- The **Sensory Room** is enjoyed particularly by our children with SEND and some of our younger pupils.

Outdoor Play and Learning (OPAL)

In primary schools, children spend up to 20%, or 1.4 years of their time in school, at play, so it's imperative that we think carefully and strategically about what is available for students during this time. We wanted to make playtimes at Flakefleet as stimulating, engaging and fun as possible.

We teamed up with OPAL (Outdoor Play and Learning) to help us do this – they're a company with expertise in developing school playgrounds and activities, with a view to improving outdoor learning.

We have made some changes to playtimes as a result of our continued work with them.

- All children across school can now access all of the school grounds at playtimes.
- We have introduced more loose parts to play with (e.g. bikes and scooters, dressing up costumes and more).
- All staff across the school have engaged in training with OPAL so we understand the different types of play and shared ideas for developing our grounds further.
- We conducted a pupil questionnaire to find out what sort of playground they would like and what activities and apparatus they would like to be brought in.

We believe that play enhances children's self-esteem and their understanding of others through freely chosen social interactions. There are also great opportunities for developing communication and negotiation skills, enabling children to develop a balance between their right to act freely and their responsibilities to others, while learning to cope with the wide range of emotions that can occur through play (including sadness, rejection, frustration, fear and boredom as well as their positive counterparts of happiness, acceptance, achievement, confidence and curiosity).

Agency

For us, agency is all about our children feeling empowered within their learning and their lives. As we've said, our school motto is #daretodream and we take that incredibly seriously at Flakefleet. We want all our children, and our staff, to feel that they have the skills and opportunities to realise their dreams and we try to commit to that in a big way.

Britain's Got Talent

In 2019, our school choir appeared on *Britain's Got Talent*, performing *Don't Stop Me Now* by Queen, and the starting point for that was one of our pupils, Megan, saying in assembly that she wanted to be on the show. The idea took hold and we decided to apply. We put an open call out to any students who wanted to be part of the choir, and tried to include as many children as we could, even those that weren't very confident singers.

We were lucky enough to win the first golden buzzer of that series, but what was even better for us was hearing the judges talk about how joyful (if chaotic) the performance was. Even though performing in that environment is scary, we didn't want our children to be scared to reach for their dreams.

Everyday practice

While we can't follow through on every individual ambition to the same degree, the principles and practice that led to this experience occur in smaller ways across our school every day.

- We talk to our children about their dreams.
- We listen carefully and commit to taking them seriously.
- We help them remove barriers to achieving those dreams.
- We normalise getting behind individual dreams as a collective: we're excited by everyone's ambition.

Spotlight profiles

At Flakefleet we want to celebrate each individual member of our community. Across the year, every pupil is chosen as a class Spotlight child for the week and positive comments from their peers and adults are shared in a celebration assembly that their family attends. This ensures that every child has an unconditional right to be celebrated by the school community for who they are – rather than whether they have 'earned' a mention through specific actions. We find this really helps build up students' self-confidence – they love hearing what the adults in the school have to say about them.

Lessons we have learned

- Adopting an **outward-facing approach** is hard work but we have found that it pays dividends in the end. Taking the time to find opportunities to engage meaningfully with our community always feels worth it.
- Embracing a **relational approach to managing behaviour** has really helped us create a calm and productive learning environment – it has benefited the children and the adults.
- We have found that we have to **keep revisiting belonging**, in the same way that we do outcomes – it is easy for it to fall off the agenda, and we have to be diligent to make sure that doesn't happen. It has to be lived and breathed every day in the school.

Time to think

Questions for reflecting on your current setting	**Questions to consider for further action**
• Where are your strongest community relationships? Describe what a strong relationship with the community looks like in your setting. • What are the biggest challenges in your community? Is the way you are tackling these in your setting in sync with wider strategies in the community? • If you were to shadow a child for a day in order to understand belonging in your school, what would you be looking for? Write down what you would use as evidence of belonging.	• How could it be made easier for your community to access your school or college? List the challenges and how they might be overcome. • If you could pick a current strategy in school to involve your wider community in, which one do you think could be strengthened the most? • If you could re-imagine or re-invent a lesser-used space in your setting, what would you pick?
Your commitment for further reflection and action 1. 2. 3.	

Time to think: Systems check

Being able to cultivate meaningful belonging in our schools is dependent on how well we understand the lived experiences of the children and adults that we work with every day.

Bronfenbrenner's ecological systems theory

Although nearly fifty years old, Bronfenbrenner's sociological theory (1979) can still be a useful way of breaking down all the interconnected factors that influence a child's growth and development.

The theory states that there are five nested environmental systems that build out from the individual and shape their unique experiences and perspectives. Each of these systems will have a bearing on the degree to which individuals feel they belong in our settings.

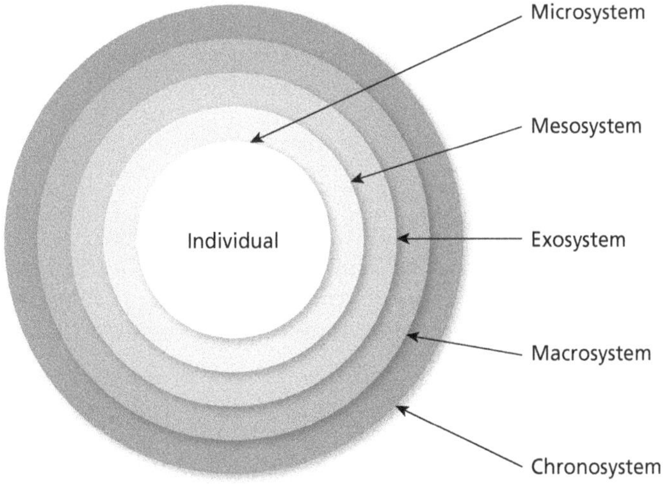

Ecological systems theory diagram

The five systems

Look at the information about each system below and spend some time reflecting on each one.

- Can you list examples for each system based on your school's context?
- How could children's (and adults') experiences of these systems impact their sense of belonging in your setting?
- What opportunities are there to strengthen a sense of belonging within each system? What system is hardest for you to consider?

There are also examples of how this links to practice shared in this book.

Microsystem

Immediate environment, relationships and daily interactions and experience. For example, at home, school, work.

- Think about explicit routines, language and behaviours that help staff provide consistency for students – such as Park Community School's Love to Teach principles (page 38), Ferndown Upper School's use of Covey's emotional bank account (page 109) and Acklam Grange School's Headspace for Learning strategy (page 74).
- Consider everyday routines and how they build connection and togetherness, such as Saracens High School's family lunch (page 3).
- Or you might want to consider processes that help every student feel recognised and valued, such as Flakefleet Primary School's Spotlight Profiles (page 19).

Mesosystem

Connections **between** microsystems. For example, connections between school, parents and the wider community.

- Examples of positive and intentional parental partnership in this book include Harmony Primary School's approach to ensuring parents feel valued and that they add value (page 84) and the parent ambassadors at King's Cross Academy (page 52).
- Consider how your school works with other local agencies, organisations and schools, such as how Saracens High School works with the Saracens rugby club (page 8), or how Deeside Sixth Form work with their feeder schools to ensure belonging from the get-go

(page 60). Flakefleet Primary School have their Strive Café (page 16), a physical space to bring school and community together.

Exosystem

Indirect influences that affect us. For example, availability of community resources, or staff workload.

- Many schools have reacted to scarcity of resource within their local community by building support into their own setting, such as Harmony Primary School's family support hub (page 90) and Park Community School's food pantry (page 37).
- Saracens High School's Making Memories Days (page 8) ensure equitable access to a range of experiences.

Macrosystem

Broader cultural context shaping all systems. For example, societal values and cultural beliefs, educational policy, and systemic inequality.

- Both Acklam Grange School (page 71) and Park Community School (page 39) have consciously worked to re-build a sense of local pride, where negative social attitudes had eroded this.
- Bantock Primary School spent time listening and learning from their families from the Gypsy, Roma and Traveller communities to re-establish trust in educational institutes (page 29). This is also central to the work of Richard Barnes Academy, who work with a number of children who have been permanently excluded from, and therefore feel rejected by, mainstream education (page 97).
- At Ferndown Upper School, they have consciously created space for boys to explore masculinity in a positive, safe and trusting environment (page 115).

Chronosystem

This time dimension, including things like life transitions, historical events (pandemic, anyone?) and societal changes that develop across a life span. This is what helps shape the different outlooks between generations.

- Park Community School's 60-year vision (page 40) helps them situate their practice within how they want to support their community in the long-term.

Bantock Primary School, Wolverhampton

Harvey Sarai, CEO
(The Wulfruna Partnership)

Jez Thomas, Headteacher

About us and our community

At Bantock Primary School, located in the heart of Wolverhampton, we serve a wonderfully diverse community of over 400 pupils, from Early Years to Year 6. We want our children to thrive at school and in the future, and for us that means having really high ambitions while also being clear-eyed about the challenges facing them, their families and our wider community.

We exist in an area of high social deprivation, with approximately 60% of our families classified as disadvantaged. Our community includes a significant proportion of new arrivals to the UK, many of whom face multiple layers of vulnerability including language barriers and limited understanding of UK systems, in addition to economic hardship. We embrace the language diversity of over 40 spoken languages and relish the opportunity to bring together cultures from around the world in our school community. The community we serve is also highly mobile, and so we experience a churn of approximately 50% year on year – this means we welcome a significant number of new children and families to our school over the course of each academic year.

As a leadership team, our work is characterised by curiosity. This means we approach every aspect of school life with a desire to understand more deeply about our children, our staff, and the community we serve.

What belonging means to us

Our aim is to ensure that all children can SHINE at Bantock. We promise a caring community where everyone can **succeed**. We provide a **happy** and exciting environment to **inspire** children to learn and grow. We **nurture** their talents and **educate** them in everything they do. We recognise, as experienced leaders, that we cannot secure the educational outcomes our children need without attending carefully to their feelings of belonging.

For us, belonging begins with really understanding our context. Like most school leaders and educators, we are deeply dedicated to public service, but it's important that we're thinking specifically about **our** public. The highly mobile nature of our community has helped shape our approach.

- We try to be proactive in understanding our community and how it is changing over time. Actively developing meaningful relationships with local leaders and families is crucial to this.
- When you have a highly mobile pupil population, you need stability in your workforce. Our staff are brilliant, and we have invested heavily in their wellbeing to ensure they feel supported.
- Our high mobility means we get to practise welcoming a lot more than many other schools. This affords us the chance to think really carefully about our induction processes and how to create moments to celebrate belonging throughout the academic year – especially for those who miss the start of the year.

Space and place

How our school looks and feels is incredibly important to us: we do a lot of welcoming, and we need our environment to communicate belonging from the first moment, particularly for those children and families who are new to the UK, some of whom may not yet speak English.

Every school building is unique and will present its own challenges to, and opportunities for, building a sense of belonging. Our building is Victorian, and so we have had to think carefully about how we can adapt and modernise the space – particularly in terms of accessibility. In an increasingly online world, we have also thought carefully about how our digital spaces can be used to build agency and foster togetherness. We have been a designated School of Sanctuary for six years, recognising our culture of welcome, inclusion and compassion for all children, especially those seeking sanctuary.

Creating a more welcoming space

- At school pick-up time, crowding on the narrow strip of pavement often saw parents forced to stand in the road while they waited for their child. We made a conscious decision to **re-do the front perimeter of the school**, moving the fenceline closer to the school and creating a more open space on the pavement. The decision was both practical and symbolic: we wanted parents to see us as a place that makes room for them.
- Once you pass our reception desk you arrive in a foyer, which we call our **Hippo Hub**. Here there is an interactive screen and soft bench seating, as well as displays celebrating our language diversity. This is where we conduct inductions for new children and families: it's in the heart of the school and in an open space. We want them to feel 'part of the school' from the outset.
- Recognising that those of us who work in the building are as much a part of the space as the architecture and displays, we are proud that **our staff body reflects the diversity of our pupil body**. It is important to us that our children can identify role models within the school community, and that many of them have the opportunity to converse with staff in their home languages.

Equitable access: Providing what is not available in the local area

We are mindful of what experiences and services are not available to all children in our community, and we try to compensate for these in school.

Libraries

There is no access to a public library in our immediate community, and so we renovated the eaves of our main school building to accommodate two libraries. These spaces are designed with a focus on creating quiet, cosy spaces as well as providing access to quality texts for all children.

Green space

Our school is surrounded on all sides by terraced housing, and there is very limited opportunity for green space on site. Despite this, part of our –

admittedly small – outdoor space is dedicated to our allotment, including a polytunnel.

Learning gardening skills, including how to grow and harvest food, provides children with opportunities to deepen their scientific knowledge while developing their social skills. Access to the polytunnel and the targeted interventions delivered there is prioritised for children whose wellbeing scores (we use the Stirling Well-Being Scale; see Liddle and Carter, 2015) indicate that they may have lower self-esteem than their peers.

Fostering calm environments

Over the years, our learning environment has been redesigned to maximise light and space and reduce sensory overwhelm.

- The **main colours throughout the building are neutral** to avoid children, and staff, being overwhelmed and overstimulated.
- We **reduced the amount of information on display boards**, streamlining these to either signpost key information or celebrate pupil learning. We have a large number of screens throughout the school and the rolling presentations they share communicate what would have once been on static displays.
- We installed **soundboards** on the ceiling of our school hall to reduce the echo from the high ceilings. We sourced a company who provided printed soundboards, so we were able to include black and white portraits of current and historical influential figures – chosen because they each represented parts of our school community or different areas of learning.

Digital spaces

As a Microsoft Showcase School, we have spent considerable time reflecting on and refining our use of technology. We believe that technology can be a really powerful lever for inclusion and belonging when deployed with care and attention.

Learning in digital spaces

Our immersive suite (with 360-degree projection) is a dedicated space that can transport children into interactive learning environments that ignite curiosity and deepen understanding. We have also used this space ahead of trips and visits for pupils who would benefit from extra advance preparation to ease nerves and anxiety.

Gathering pupil voice

Our website also provides a 'digital safe space' for children.

- They can submit a 'worry' that comes through as an email to the headteacher. At a time that is suitable, the headteacher will discuss the concerns with the child, ensuring they feel heard.
- Alternatively, children can share good news through our 'happy box', which is always acknowledged by the headteacher and earns the child a special sticker.

You'll notice in the examples that children are prompted to reflect on the source of their emotions, and what would help them (in the case of worries).

Worry box	Happy box
I am feeling sad **because** my grandma died. **I would feel better if** she was never dead. **I am feeling** uneasy **because** my friend decided to write a bad message on Minecraft Education and I forgot to tell the teacher. **I would feel better if** anyone could comfort me as I have social anxiety.	**I am feeling** grateful and carefree **because** I know it is a little bit late, but I have been eager to tell you that I love the changes to the school that you made such as the library, the hall icons and the school medical changes. I wish we would have these changes more often because they really make me feel more positive about learning and make me feel more fulfilled when walking around the school.

Examples of worry box and happy box messages

It's important to note that these digital mechanisms – which are well used by our children – are only effective because of the quality of the relationships that we have with our children offline.

Relations

Relationships are crucial in all settings. We want to understand our community well: only by doing that can we know best how we can help and support them. Because of the highly mobile nature of our community, we need to build relationships quickly and understand how the demographics of our community are changing over time.

The importance of induction

The way in which we welcome and initiate new members of our school community is vital for laying the foundations for positive relationships. It's important for all families, especially those who are new to the area or country. For many of our parents and children, our school is the first official UK institution that they have engaged with. We don't want to make any assumptions about what parents know about how our school, and the English school system, works.

Over the years, we have tweaked and refined our induction process (and continue to do so).

- We host family inductions in the Hippo Hub, which has been specifically designed to **celebrate the diversity** within our school. We communicate clearly that we believe the diversity of our community strengthens us.
- We provide **clear visuals** wherever possible: for example, simple bird's-eye view maps of the school building to show where drop-off and pick-up is, and examples of the school uniform modelled on mannequins to visually display uniform expectations.
- Where members of our community can provide interpretation into home languages, we try to provide this, sometimes helped by our parent ambassadors. We use subtitle settings in PowerPoints too, both in English and in different home languages.
- We clearly signpost the school website as a digital platform for sharing information, including a number of videos that introduce different aspects of our learning environment.

For our new arrivals, to help ensure a smooth transition into school life we do not academically assess children in the first two weeks of arrival at school: the focus is firmly on friendships, routines, basic vocabulary and social and emotional wellbeing.

Leading with curiosity: Building relationships with our GRT families

With some families and communities there was a legacy of generalised mistrust of education institutes and so we had to go back and try to rebuild relationships. We have a higher than national average proportion of students from Gypsy, Roma and Traveller (GRT) families, especially

Roma. In line with national trends, we were finding that families from GRT communities did not always feel comfortable in our school, which was affecting attendance and achievement – but most importantly it was affecting their sense of belonging. We invested a lot of time into researching Roma communities so that we understand their history and culture.

The relationships we built by doing this work led to recruiting our very first parent ambassadors, giving parents an authentic and trusted voice within school. The impact of this role along with other strategic initiatives (for example, the changes we have made to parents' evenings) has resulted in higher than national average attendance of GRT pupils.

There is also evidence that parents are trusting us more. Historically, our parents from GRT communities have been reluctant to give permission for their children to attend school trips; while challenges still remain in this area, we are pleased that the majority of our GRT children attend school trips and have even attended our four-day residential trip in Year 6.

The creation of the parent ambassador role has also now expanded across the school, with a growing number of parents working alongside us to strengthen our understanding of, and links to, the communities we serve. As a direct result of their work as a parent ambassador, one individual completed a social care degree. They have remained working at our school because they could see how their work mattered and how they were adding value.

Parents' evenings as a community event

Over the years, we have re-shaped parents' evenings into a community event. We wanted to capitalise on times when we have parents in the building and make the interaction as meaningful as possible.

As well as having important conversations with their teachers, parents can also access a range of services to support them as well as more information about school initiatives. Parents' evenings often include:

- Samples of lunches.
- Digital and IT support, as well as access to the school nurse.
- Book fairs.
- Local community groups – such as the Wolves Foundation.

Not only has parental attendance at parents' evenings increased from 70% to nearly 90%, the attendance of our parents from GRT communities has increased from 26% to 80% over the years. We have found that the open, supportive and genuinely helpful offer at parents' evenings has changed the character of the relationship that we have with many of our families.

Low-stakes engagement

While the large events such as parents' evening are brilliant opportunities to bring our community together, we also recognise the importance of everyday interactions in building quality relationships.

- As a leadership team we are on the gate every morning and every afternoon to greet parents. Parents know they will have the opportunity to chat to us if they have any concerns and this negates the need for separate meetings during and after the school day. It also allows us to respond quickly when necessary.
- Our regular **parent chatter** sessions respond to the needs in the parent community as they arise. Sessions in the past have focused on diet and nutrition, online safety, SATs, phonics and ESOL classes. Because parents are comfortable in our school environment, we have also been able to bring them in for expert sessions that go beyond the education sphere – providing parents with the opportunity to get advice and guidance in a warm and familiar setting. For example, we have led a session with a solicitor's firm to support families who were concerned about their legal rights to remain in the country after Brexit.

One parent recently passed on this feedback: 'Bantock is a great school of learning for children of different backgrounds. Great learning experiences and parental engagement and communication. Teachers … exhibit great professionalism and mutual respect to all parents.'

Agency

School comes alive when members of our community – children, staff and parents – are active participants within school life and within their learning. As one pupil put it, 'The teachers dig out the deepest curiosity inside you. We explore our learning as if we're exploring a jungle.'

Emotional regulation

For us, self-reflection and self-regulation are the bedrock of agency, and we are explicit about equipping our children with these skills.

We are a UNICEF Rights Respecting School, and both our behaviour and health and wellbeing policies encourage a process that enables children to reflect on the root causes of issues, understand their responsibilities to themselves and the wider community, and understand the impact of their choices. Through a consistent and scaffolded approach, children are invited to consider appropriate consequences and identify alternative solutions when managing a problem.

Pupil voice and responsibility

Children have an active voice at Bantock, and real responsibility.

- We have a wide variety of ambassador roles for pupils. These include: sports, digital, media, rights respecting and Minecraft ambassadors. Children receive training for these roles – sometimes internally and sometimes externally. For example, our digital ambassadors work with our technology partners, Concero UK.
- Our pupils are actively involved in our programme of assemblies, presenting on a whole range of themes and issues determined by themselves.
- The **ideas box** on our website allows pupils to submit ideas for school improvement. The idea for this in itself came from a child. Recently children requested more plants in the playground area, which we have worked to deliver despite the constraints of our environment.

Our agency as leaders

It's also really important to us that we are modelling agency and continual improvement for our children and our staff. We actively seek out external awarding processes – some of which we have mentioned here, such as the Carnegie Centre of Excellence Gold Mental Health Award, Parent-Friendly Schools Accreditation, Rights Respecting Schools Gold Award, being a Microsoft Showcase school and being a designated School of Sanctuary.

We don't do this so that we can collect certificates and awards (although we do, and you will see them proudly displayed throughout our school). Rather, it's so that we know that we are constantly providing ourselves with challenge and a framework against which we can test our current practice and strive to improve.

Especially for communities like ours, which can be under-served nationally, it's important to us that we are relentless in seeking out opportunities to improve for the benefit of all the children we are privileged to educate.

Lessons we have learned

- **Controlling what we can control and accepting what we can't.** We always endeavour to have a positive, appreciative outlook. While we wish things were easier for many of our families, we serve them best by focusing on what we as a school **can** help with.
- **Delaying action in favour of understanding.** We prioritise understanding our community and the families we serve. Taking time to do this before we act often means we are able to act more radically.
- **Always revisiting embedded practice.** Because communities, contexts and needs are always changing, we embrace the fact that we will never be 'done'. We're really proud of the work that we have done so far, but we know that we will need to continually revisit and tweak our practice in response to a community and profession that is always changing.

Time to think

Questions for reflecting on your current setting	Questions to consider for further action
• Reflect on your community over the last ten years. How has it changed? Have your approaches adapted in line with these? • Think about your physical environment. List all the things that signal 'there is space for you here.' Now do the same for your digital environments. What do you notice? • What systems and processes do you already have in place for revisiting embedded practice? Can any of these be adapted or tweaked to help you reflect on your practice in relation to belonging?	• Think about the different groups that make up your wider community. Which groups do you know the least about? Which cultures are not represented within your staff body, for example? How can you learn more? • Spend some time quickly jotting down the challenges facing your local community. Notice how specific you are able to be. Then go through the list of challenges and highlight in **green** where your setting is currently supporting, and in **yellow** where your setting could support. Which challenge could you start planning to overcome? Revisit this regularly – things will change.

Your commitment for further reflection and action
1.
2.
3.

Park Community School, Hampshire

Chris Anders, Headteacher

Ella Capaldi, Head of School

About us and our community

We are an over-subscribed maintained secondary school based in Havant, a few miles north of Portsmouth. The school is located in the centre of what was once Europe's largest housing estate – Leigh Park. Despite being in Hampshire, our school is not a 'typical' Hampshire school. Many of our children and families experience poverty and we work hard at Park to mitigate the effect of this on learning.

We take our role as a community school seriously. We are proud to serve at the heart of our community, and we are open until late seven days a week, 51 weeks a year. In addition to our main school site, we operate a number of off-site bases that serve our community while also providing diverse experiences for our children and young people. These include a smallholding on a local farm, a print business in an industrial unit, a construction skills centre in an old ambulance station and a tearoom in our local country park. Many staff used to be children at this school, and we employ current students in a variety of roles, whenever possible using training routes to turn passion into a career.

What belonging means to us

At Park, we work to create and celebrate pride in belonging to our community. Historically, negative perceptions of Leigh Park from those outside our community have impacted how our children and families perceive themselves, their abilities and the opportunities available to them. We talk intentionally about being **proud to be a part of Park**. That is not just about being proud to be part of our school, but about being proud of being from the wider community. That's why we are always on the look-out for opportunities to deepen our ties with our local community: to bring the community into the school, and for the school to extend out into the community.

We want young people to **find what they love** to do, enabling them to lead a satisfying life and play a full part in our community. Our curriculum, including our extra-curricular offer, is broad in order to provide the greatest chance of our young people finding the thing that lights them up and having space to explore that. In particular, our **Much More Than Just A School** carousel curriculum aims to provide students with unique opportunities to participate in a range of valuable experiences outside of the classroom, and our off-site locations are key to helping us facilitate this.

Our school's vision aims to address two existential challenges facing young people: learning to cope with angst and learning to make good choices. Our ambition is that Park helps our young people find lifelong purpose and passion: cultivating a sense of belonging is crucial to achieving this.

Space and place

For us, attending to space and place is about how we use our physical location – on- and off-site – to provide students with those meaningful, real-world experiences, while also serving our wider community as best we can.

In the early noughties, the Labour government had a goal for schools to become community hubs through extending opening hours. This intention never manifested into practice, despite an implementation target of 2010 – but that did not mean it was not a worthwhile or important aspiration for a school to be at the centre of its community. We have worked to make this a reality at Park. We are open throughout the year, even for lunch on Christmas Day. We believe schools are important community assets and spaces for bringing people together: we try to keep ours open.

What follows are some of the ways that we have tried to strengthen our ties to, and support for, our community through commercial enterprise and local partnerships.

Investment

Cuts to funding for community activities at Park Community School in the early years of the coalition government reduced our funding for opening out of school hours by around £40k. We were committed to being a community hub and so we had to think commercially to replace the lost funding.

People

We sought new local groups and clubs to increase the use of the school buildings and facilities in the evenings and weekends. That meant an investment in staff: we could not choose between having either a member of site team or a receptionist, because we needed both if we wanted to be busier. This investment set into motion a positive cycle: the more staff we employed, the more lettings we could have, and the more employment opportunities we created. We prioritised recruiting recent school leavers for these positions.

Facilities

Between 2011 and 2015 the school was largely rebuilt and the remaining third was refurbished. There was a trade-off here: we largely lost our community business for two years during this time, but our potential for revenue increased. We increased the number of large spaces available – including a number of flexible classrooms and a new theatre with double the capacity of our previous one. Continual investment in the lighting, sound equipment and technical support means that our theatre is busy many weekends through the year, which again creates work and training opportunities for young people.

Scale is crucial for a school to work as a business, and that business in turn helps to ensure quality facilities for school children through the higher levels of staffing in the school day made possible by the higher level of income.

Busy evenings on our 3G football pitch allows income to be saved in a 'sinking fund'. That means we will be ready to resurface the pitch when it needs replacing. At a cost of over £200k, this is beyond the scope of a normal school budget, but without it the surface might only have a 15-year life span.

A place of employment as well as learning

Opening up to our community has allowed us to employ many former and current students over the years. Young people are employed as receptionists, site support, party hosts, theatre technicians and members of our catering team. Being a community hub means we run, and so need support for, holiday activity programmes. During the school holidays, up to fifty students work at school (even more if you include our former students).

Before employment, students need to apply, be interviewed and secure the job. Not all are successful. Employment also means that we sometimes need to help students set up bank accounts, which of course requires birth certificates and the completion of paperwork - all useful, practical experiences for them to take into their futures. Students also learn about working life through purposeful conversations with the school staff training and leading them.

Employing students alongside our own site team not only leads to better decoration and less litter, it helps students see that school is about more than just the obvious things. It gives greater scope for experiencing success and understanding the intrinsic value in contributing - all of which underpins belonging at Park.

Catering for our community

Food is important - not only for nutrition, but for demonstrating care and building a shared culture. In 2014 we made the decision to bring our catering in-house and set up a catering business, employing a professional chef to work collaboratively with us. This has not only improved the quality of the food we serve but has also provided opportunities to develop our young people and to support our communities.

Our chefs have won national awards and have even catered at 10 Downing Street, showing the Prime Minister and his guests just how good school food can be - they turned school dinners into canapés for an event overseen by Jamie Oliver to promote higher food standards in schools.

Skills development for young people

Our catering students get real-world experience in our school kitchens, working alongside our professional team. Flexibility as well as scale means that the school kitchen is busy during the holidays, and we have been able to employ half a dozen school leavers as apprentice chefs.

We partner with Hampshire County Council's Countryside Service to operate a tearoom in the local country park. Our tearoom is a commercial venture to help support our various charitable catering activities.

Supporting families and individuals experiencing hardship

We are able to open earlier for breakfast in term-time. We work with Magic Breakfast to provide a free healthy breakfast to any who want it. In 2017, we began Munch – with a small amount of funding from a local councillor – to provide lunches throughout the school holidays. Ultimately, this developed into a foodbank and then a pantry, where food can be offered at significantly less than cost through charitable giving (both large and small), the National Lottery and government grants.

Authentic learning environments

Our wider curriculum offer aims to ensure students experience a broad range of learning in and outside the classroom and connect this to the real world. One part of this is our Much More Than Just A School carousel. Every student in Years 7, 8 and 9 spends time in our media suite creating podcasts, at our print shop working on an enterprise project, in our kitchen helping to prepare our meals, at our smallholding focusing on horticulture and caring for our pigs, and at our construction skills centre experiencing practical skills such as plastering and brick laying.

We have built learning opportunities around what we already do as a school and where we can develop small businesses to create opportunities for work experience (both paid and unpaid). Our onsite nursery cares for around 50 babies and pre-school children, and our students studying childcare can gain important practical experience here. Away from school we have a print business in a local industrial unit – we do our school printing here but about 60% of the work is external, coming from our wider community.

Relations

At Park, we love to teach (and 'we' means **everyone**). We believe every moment in and out of the classroom can help students find what they love, and so we aim to provide a wide range of adults and role models with whom they can connect, build relationships, and be supported and challenged by. Because every moment counts, we sweat the small stuff – we are explicit about how we want to demonstrate to our children and young people that we value them.

Our Love to Teach principles

These underpin all our relationships at Park. They are based on our belief that for students to thrive they must feel a strong sense of belonging and experience a balance of challenge and support.

- Welcome me.
- Inspire me.
- Challenge me.
- Invest in me.
- Model passion for Park.

All 175 of our staff know and model these principles. As leadership, we explicitly and simply define and summarise them for staff. They are deliberately articulated in the voice of the student, demonstrating our belief that these are things every child is entitled to at Park. We will explain the first and fifth principles in more detail here, and return to the others in the Agency section when we discuss pedagogy.

Model passion for Park

Despite coming last on the list, this is our underpinning principle. In every action and interaction, we aim to show that we are proud to be part of our school and our community. We want to let our students know that we, as adults, are happy to be here, and we are happy that they are here too.

Welcome me

This is about making sure that every child feels seen and included at Park. We deliberately take time to get to know every child, welcome them into school every day and interact positively throughout the day – in corridors and in our restaurant, as well as in our classrooms.

Our 'Welcome me' descriptors include things that sound obvious: know my name, smile at me, give me positive eye contact and body language, always let me have a fresh start.

Most staff in most schools would do these things naturally, but by listing them like this and reminding ourselves of our commitment to them it helps everyone stay on the same page even on the toughest days. This also means there is consistency across all our staff, including those with roles that are not typically as student-facing as teachers. Our deliberate development of this starts when any new staff interview with us and become formalised through staff induction.

The outcome of this is that every day our children have multiple interactions with many adults who are happy to see them and let them know this explicitly.

Our place in the world

We have spoken already about how important our local community relationships are. For some of our children, the opportunity to travel is limited and so we focus explicitly on helping students understand and connect with the world beyond our immediate community.

International experiences

We have done a lot of work over the last few years on increasing students' international experiences, and the impact of those experiences, framed within our theme of 'our place in the world'.

We have worked with an organisation to facilitate over 120 Chinese students visiting Park for week-long immersions into school over five separate visits. Year 8 students apply to be buddies with the visiting students and throughout the week they share with each other their experiences of growing up in the UK and China. This not only helps foster curiosity, cultural understanding and inspire exploration, but also, because of the two-way nature of the visit, students are not only learning from their visitors, they are also teaching about their own experiences, which helps build self-esteem and confidence.

We have used the Turing scheme (Department for Education, 2025) to build on the experience, taking 20 Year 9 students to a university in India in 2025. This year, we repeated this visit along with a 10-day trip to Chinese schools for Year 10 students, and a 10-day trip to Gwalior and Jaipur schools in India for Year 10 and 11.

While only approximately 10% of the year group are able to study internationally, the immersion programme that we have built around the trips and the way we share these experiences has helped everyone at Park feel part of the experience.

Parks around the globe

One much simpler way we connect our everyday experience at school to the wider world is through the naming of different wings in our school after national parks from around the world: Yellowstone, Jau, Cairngorms, Sagarmatha, Kruger, Galapagos and Machu Picchu.

Long-term relationships

As a school, we are committed to growing and nourishing long-term relationships with our community. We have a 60-year vision, in which we look forward to meeting parents who valued their education at our school

– those who have happy memories of learning and life in the compulsory stages of education and are ready to support us when it matters: they value the school and education it offers over the immediate wishes (or moans) of their children. 28 years into the 60-year timeframe that we have set, we are seeing this relationship with the school from more and more of our parents. This approach helps us prioritise decisions that are going to serve our young people – and community – best in the long term.

Agency

We have an unwavering focus at Park on preparing our young people for life beyond school. Academic qualifications that open doors for their next steps are part of that, but so is ensuring that our young people are resilient, active contributors and able to make good choices. At Park, we call this having autonomy. And if we want it for our children, it has to start with us as leaders.

Sticking to our vision

One of the (many) challenges of being a school leader is how to deliver meaningful educational outcomes for our children that make them feel successful, knowing that the system in which we operate does not allow for all children to succeed. We know that, because of norm- rather than criterion-referenced grading, a significant number of children will and must fail their exams every year. The system makes it so. It also prioritises short-term goals and metrics over long-term vision and transformation.

So for us at Park we try hard to prioritise what we think will make the long-term difference to individuals and the community, knowing that what we do is often not valued by policy makers, but is valued by our parents and community. That's why our curriculum has such a strong focus on helping children find what they love – whatever that is. Of course, GCSEs are important at Park, but we also deliver other qualifications that we believe to be important – even ones that do not count in league table statistics.

Star Curriculum

Our Star Curriculum is a transdisciplinary curriculum designed to enable students to connect learning authentically and taught to the whole of Year 7 for 50% of their timetable. The curriculum was inspired by the New Basics model of Queensland, Australia (Matters, *et al.*, 2004) and focuses on removing the artificial separation between subjects and developing connections and transferable skills, making learning more authentic, and directly applying this to the real world. It is underpinned by literacy, oracy and critical thinking.

The number of teachers delivering our Star Curriculum is limited to a team who applied specifically for the role and experienced training in the pedagogy of this approach to learning. Each group of 25–30 students is taught by either one or two Star teachers in one base classroom. Assessment opportunities include a series of Rich Challenges designed to require students to apply their learning to different and authentic situations for real audiences. The Rich Challenges are assessed against a set of competencies and recorded in digital portfolios that have been inspired by 'rethinking assessment' (Rethinking Assessment, n.d.).

A recent example of a Rich Challenge was an identity exhibition. The theme of identity and local history has been the focus for learning this term and culminated in students creating oral histories of the area using local people as inspiration and presenting these in a travelling exhibition. The exhibition was initially displayed in school, where parents and families were invited to experience it and the children had the opportunity to teach the audience about their learning. It then moved on to our tea rooms, a local theatre and the library, before returning to the main school for community viewing.

Support and challenge in the classroom

Our Love to Teach principles include three that focus specifically on teaching and pedagogy: Inspire me, Challenge me and Invest in me. They aim to ensure that our classrooms are both challenging and supportive, based on Vygotsky's zones of proximal development, which we refer to as comfort, stretch and challenge (Vygotsky, 1978).

The expectation is that students are in the stretch zone for new learning, and the teacher helps students move from one zone to the next and back again. By frequently returning to the comfort zone, then back to stretch with increasing challenge each time, students' confidence and skills build. We teach students that getting stuck is a good thing, and developing strategies to help them overcome any panic they may feel so that they can move back to stretch is all part of the learning process – not an individual failure.

Making good choices

Ensuring that young people know how to make good choices for themselves and are able to take responsibility for their actions is a big part of developing agency and autonomy.

Our behaviour policy talks about making good choices and making poor choices. Our approach helps students understand how poor choices impact others, and staff are trained to help refocus behaviour and encourage good choices. Our boundaries for good and poor choices are very clearly communicated to students, which helps us maintain a supportive environment while not compromising on our expectations.

Through repeated reference to choices rather than a focus on consequences we want our students to learn that they are responsible for their actions.

Lessons we have learned

- Have a **long-term vision** for what you want in your school, with clear guiding principles that underpin it. This helps cut through the noise of changing trends and acts as a guiding star for decision-making.
- Be **open to opportunities**. Finding the first opportunity and making a start requires some bravery and financial investment.
- Develop **deep, multi-generational relationships**. This cannot happen quickly, and it does require us to be deliberate. It also needs colleagues who want to give most, or all, of a 40-year career to the school.

Time to think

Questions for reflecting on your current setting	**Questions to consider for further action**
• Think about all the ways that pride is demonstrated and modelled to your students. What are the behaviours that elicit 'I'm proud of you.' or 'You should be proud of yourself.' from staff? • Are you aware of what barriers (individual, local, systemic) might be negatively impacting on positive self-regard, self-efficacy and self-confidence in your setting? Who are the students that have been on the biggest journey of growth in this area? What helped facilitate that? • What opportunities are there in your setting for students to learn about the intrinsic value of contributing?	• What is your 60-year vision for your school and local community? What are the biggest differences between now and then? • Which subjects or departments already have success with using authentic learning environments to help students connect their learning to the real world? Are there curriculum areas that might benefit from more of this? What opportunities are there in your local area to connect learning to authentic experiences? • What is important to you as a leader, that is not (currently) important to policy makers? How do you protect this and ensure it remains a guiding star in your decision-making?
Your commitment for further reflection and action 1. 2. 3.	

Time to think: Child development and belonging

Belonging is important for all of us, at all stages of our lives, but when we're thinking about supporting children and young people in education settings their age and developmental stage will have a large bearing on what they need from us in order to foster a secure sense of belonging.

This is a quick whistle-stop tour and requires us to deal in very broad brushstrokes. There will, of course, be a lot more nuance when we look at individual children and contexts.

Developmental stage	Secure belonging characteristics
Early childhood	• Emotional safety. • Predictable and consistent routines. • Caring teacher relationships.
Middle childhood	• Peer connections, including a growing sense of personal reputation. • Inclusive classroom communities. • Recognition of competence within the classroom.
Adolescence	• A clear sense of identity that is formed in part by membership of groups. • Ability to be autonomous and independent. • Making meaningful contributions. • Relationships with trusted adults.

Simplified secure belonging developmental journey (supportive literature for this table includes Allen, 2020; Battistich and Hom, 1997; Bronfenbrenner, 1979; Goodenow and Grady, 1993; Haun and Tomasello, 2011; Osterman, 2000; Over, 2016; Walton and Cohen, 2011)

Implications for school settings

Of course, emotional safety does not become less important for adolescents, and inclusive classrooms that allow all students to experience success will be beneficial at all ages. The journey from early childhood to adolescence can be characterised as one towards a solidified sense of social identity – 'who we are' – and it is informed by our membership to groups.

Regardless of which age group we work with primarily, we may want to consider the questions below.

- How do we cultivate emotional safety, including emotional literacy to support self-expression?

  For example, Bantock Primary School's support for emotional regulation (page 31), Acklam Grange School's Headspace for Learning strategy (page 38), Richard Barnes Academy's therapeutic approach (page 103) or Ferndown Upper School's co-curated safe spaces (page 114).

- How do we model and scaffold cooperation and inclusion?

  For example, the positive approaches to restorative conversations at Flakefleet Primary School (page 13) and Ferndown Upper School (page 111), student involvement in target setting at Harmony Primary School (page 83) or student and staff cooperation being made explicit in the daily routines at Richard Barnes Academy (page 99).

- How do we promote positive social norms?

  For example, Park Community School's emphasis on 'making good choices' (page 42), how Acklam Grange's Pride Pod encourages students to take pride in their work (page 74), or how changes made to the physical environment at Deeside 6th support desired learning behaviours (page 66).

- How do we provide a wide variety of opportunities (and groups) for students to explore?

  For example, the inclusive curriculum approach taken at King's Cross Academy (page 51), Park Community School's Star Curriculum (page 41), and Saracens High School's 'Making Memories Days' (page 8).

- How do we promote collaboration within and beyond the classroom?

  For example, the emphasis at Park Community School on authentic learning environments (page 38), Flakefleet Primary School's focus on outdoor playtime provision (page 18) and Harmony Primary School's family learning workshops.

- How do we create opportunities for children and young people to make meaningful contributions?

  For example, King's Cross Academy's emphasis on and care and commitment to 'who you are not what you achieve' (page 49), Bantock Primary School's pupil leadership with real responsibility (page 32) and Deeside 6th's work on legacy (page 65).

Transition

Understanding the changing emphasis of belonging – and the threats to it – as children move through our school system can help us be proactive and pre-emptive, particularly around key transitions (which can pose a risk to belonging in and of itself). The 'Year 7 dip' in pupil happiness, engagement and sense of belonging is well-documented, with one in four pupils disengaging from school in the first year of secondary school (ImpactEd Group, 2025).

If you feel like being collaborative, you may want to explore the considerations above with colleagues from schools and settings that your students transition into/out of. Understanding the practice that students experience before and after their time with you may provide opportunities to deepen and adapt your own practice.

Or, if you would prefer to reflect on your own, spend some time thinking about the developmental journey.

- Think about the age that students are when they transition **into** your setting. How does your practice during transition align with the belonging needs for that age group?
- Now think about the age that students are when they transition **out of** your setting. How is your practice preparing them for their next steps?

King's Cross Academy, London

Dr Stephen Mitchell, Headteacher

About us and our community

King's Cross Academy (KCA) is a primary school (EYFS to Year 6) that has been open for ten years. Our building sits in the heart of the King's Cross estate redevelopment, which is a major hub for technology and creative industries, housing the offices of companies such as Google, Meta, Sony, Nike and AstraZeneca.

Our children, however, don't come from this immediate locality and instead join us from all over Camden. That means that, while in some ways we are incredibly privileged to be situated where we are, we do not have a ready-made community or an obvious catchment area.

Since the school first opened, our community has shifted – from the first pioneering group of families who were heavily involved in the creation of the school (along with my predecessor) to a cohort that more accurately represents Camden as a whole. Camden is an interesting part of London because there are more school places than there are children, and so you often find families 'voting with their feet' and moving schools if they don't like something the school is doing. On the flip side, social housing in Camden is very competitive and so, generally, those of our families that qualify for it will often have intersecting and compounding vulnerabilities such as special educational needs or disability, socioeconomic hardship, and significant safeguarding concerns.

Despite the very real challenges many of our families navigate with resilience and determination, our community is defined far more by its warmth, ambition and deep commitment to children than by any barriers it faces. It is a community that looks out for one another and holds high aspirations for every child.

What belonging means to us

We are incredibly aware that the affluence on display in our immediate surroundings does not reflect the lived experiences of the vast majority of our children and their families. For us at KCA, a core part of our focus on belonging has been about resolving the dissonance of that fact: we want our children to feel that they belong not only in our school, but alongside the success and innovation that the estate represents.

Since I joined the school as headteacher three years ago, we have had a strong focus on both building on the authentic connection that has always existed between the school and its community, while also creating systems and processes that bring clarity, consistency and transparency to our practice.

We try always to be a listening school: we want the voices of our teachers, our pupils, our parents and our wider community to be heard. We have been working over the last three years on ways to do that fairly and clearly.

Our children are, quite simply, the jewel in the crown of the King's Cross Estate – and everything we do is rooted in ensuring they flourish, feel valued and are given every opportunity to thrive.

Relations

The quality of the relationships underpins everything that happens in school and determines how willing and able individuals feel to show up authentically as themselves. Our aim is that every child and every adult in our school feels that we take the time to understand their unique attributes. Whether or not two individuals perfectly hit it off cannot be guaranteed, and so we try to underpin our relational practice with routines and systems that we can fall back on.

Every child is known

For children to feel that they belong in our school, they need to feel that we genuinely know and care about them. While staff will, of course, do a lot instinctively and intuitively to get to know their children, these are some of the ways that we have been working on to bring consistency so that no child is forgotten, and this is driven from SLT.

Daily SLT classroom visits

Our aim, across the team, is to pop in and say hello in every classroom, every day. While we can't always do this in practice, we make a point of stepping out onto the playground, or out into the corridors, to be visible to the children in the school.

SLT meetings

Our weekly SLT meetings will have one of three focuses – attendance, safeguarding or pastoral – and will look specifically at one year group each week. As an SLT team we go through every child in relation to those focus areas. That means that every single child is spoken about by the leadership team, three times per half term with three distinct perspectives. This ensures that all of us have our eyes on all the children and helps us be proactive and intervene early where necessary.

School improvement plan

A central part of our school improvement plan is that we know at least one genuine hobby or interest for every child. We believe that when a child discovers something they care deeply about, it strengthens their sense of identity and significantly increases the likelihood that they will remain engaged in education over time.

This principle underpins our ongoing curriculum development. To achieve this goal, we deliberately expose children to a wide range of experiences. We aim to broaden horizons and expand possibilities, so that every child has the opportunity to discover their unique passion – the spark that motivates them.

Celebrating who you are not what you achieve

It's important to us that our children believe that we care about the people that they are, not just what they achieve in their lessons. Like many schools, we have a variety of award schemes to recognise our children in different ways. We always try to praise the process, not the outcome.

- Our **House points** are linked to demonstrating positive learning behaviours, not for a learning outcome. The winning House is rewarded with a substantial prize each term (a cinema trip, an adventure play park visit or utilising some of the opportunities on the King's Cross Estate).
- **Star of the week** is awarded to children for showing one of our school rules in action.

- **Headteacher's Tea Party** happens each half term and is for two pupils in every class who have shown dedication towards their learning. This might be linked to an improvement in attendance, or an increased work ethic, depending on the child.
- **Book vending machine credits** are awarded every half term to children who demonstrate outstanding levels of effort in regard to their reading, writing or maths learning.

We track all of these things meticulously so that we can anticipate which children might be less visible and find opportunities to shine a light on them. All children should be celebrated at least once a year.

Consistency and clarity

We believe that being clear and consistent is the bedrock of building trust – whether that be between staff members, with children or with parents.

- We have **consistent routines** across the staff for how we do certain things – for example the way we count down to silence and the way in which we structure learning across the day.
- All staff are trained in and understand **how to handle difficult conversations**. As a leadership team, we are explicit about how we want the conversation to look and feel when things aren't going well – we have structured vocabulary frames for different levels of intervention that we are all expected to use.
- **During staff recruitment**, we are very transparent about the way we do things at KCA, so that staff can decide if we are the right fit for them based on our ethos and approach.
- We ask parents to sign a **parent partnership agreement** that clearly states what the school is going to do for the child, and what we ask from the parent in return. In its most simple form, it boils down to: if they come to parents' evenings and engage with the school across the year, we will provide their child with opportunities they will not need to pay for. This is underpinned by a clear system and process that staff can use if things go off track.

Agency

It is our ambition to fill our children full of confidence in their abilities and attributes. Everything we do in school has a global intention of instilling a sense of positivity and self-efficacy in our pupils. Our ambition for pupils in Year 6 is that they leave KCA with a strong sense of themselves and what they are genuinely interested in to take forward to secondary school (especially as our catchment means that our pupils go on to a very wide variety of different secondary schools).

Our curriculum

We want all our children to find opportunities to shine within our curriculum, and from the outset parents and staff were keen that the curriculum had a strong emphasis on the foundation subjects, especially the arts as a way to open up worlds and give children tools for self-expression, exploration and curiosity. We want children to have as many opportunities as possible to uncover their unique learning aptitudes and gifts.

SATs results provide a narrow view of a child's abilities. We try to ensure that every child has the opportunity to demonstrate their learning beyond the core curriculum.

- Children learn Level 1 British Sign Language as part of their time with us. This is delivered in conjunction with our co-located school, Frank Barnes School for Deaf Children.
- All Year 3 children do London Academy of Music and Dramatic Art qualifications in speaking in public, which improves their confidence and oracy at a vital point in their education journey. (LAMDA, 2026)
- We have a minimum expectation that every child will learn to play an instrument, and we have invested time and resource into making this a reality.

You'll notice that these are available for all children. If we are committed to equity – and we like to think that we are! – we do not want to have any opt-in, paid-for elements of our wider curriculum and enrichment offer. We believe that if something is worth doing then it is worth paying for all the children to be able to do it – not only those whose families are willing or able to pay for it. This means that our school trip abroad, which we do every year, is funded for all children. In 2026/27, every child in Year 6 is going to have the opportunity to join us in France.

Choosing role models and leaders

Pupil parliament

Our pupil parliament is made up of 15 children from Reception to Year 6. Members are selected in annual general elections by their peers, following speeches that are made in response to a 'big question' that is linked to an element of school life that pupils are passionate about (usually for our children this is related to food or play!).

House mascots

Pupils also vote for who they want their House mascots to be, giving them the opportunity to choose their own role models. At the time of writing, our role models are Malala Yousafzai, David Attenborough and Marcus Rashford. We think it's important that children are given the opportunity to decide for themselves who their role models can be – and the fact that we change them every year, alongside our general elections for pupil parliament, means that children are exposed to a wide diversity of role models, not just one person for their entire journey in school.

Class names

Our classes are named after local, living artists such as Bea Bonini and Yinka Shonibare. We want the arts to feel close and connected to our children's lives, and the ambition is that these artists will come and run creative arts projects with our children (although this is still a work in progress). We want them to have a real experience of what being an artist **today** looks like, not just what it was like centuries ago.

Parent agency

When the school began, as we've mentioned, there was a lot of agency felt by that first pioneering group of parents. This is something that we have been keen to preserve and build on, and has led to our formalised structure of parent representatives.

Every class in our school has a designated parent rep from the community. As a school, we do not get involved in the selection and to be honest we don't even know what the process for selection is: it is entirely owned by the parents. As headteacher, I email and say 'I would like to know who your class rep is by Friday', and on Friday there are 15 emails with 15 names.

WhatsApp communication

Each parent rep is then in a WhatsApp group with me as Head (on a work phone). This is a really valuable and effective stream of two-way communication. It allows me to get fast, direct feedback from parents on announcements and initiatives and has led to the school being able to diffuse tension quickly. We have a very clear understanding and protocol about what we do and do not discuss in the chat: the parents appreciate that they have direct access to school leadership, and as a result it is not abused. It's important to note that this works because of the generally positive relationships that we have with our parent community – it certainly wouldn't have been my first move as Head, but it works for us now.

There are other parent WhatsApp groups for each class, which all parents are invited to join if they would like to. That's also been a really good way of welcoming new families to the school community, especially as our children come from all over the borough and most families will not know each other outside of school.

At-home learning

We have spent a lot of time thinking about homework. We want the work children do at home to be meaningful, but we also want it to be something that parents are happy with and able to support. This has led to us changing our homework policy quite significantly.

No academic learning happens at home. Instead, homework is based around six pieces of work per half term that can be done in any order. Some pieces of work take just five minutes and others take up to two hours, but pupils and parents can decide themselves when they want to do each piece so that it fits in best with home. Some examples of pieces of work are completing a poem based on their class learning or designing and building their own London landmark. To support this, every child in Years 3–6 is provided with a Chromebook and dongle to ensure good internet access.

Space and place

The location of our school means that we have some quite unique challenges and opportunities when it comes to our environment. On the one hand, very few of our parents will work or live around the corner from our school, which can make it hard for them to feel 'at home' in our physical community. There are also limitations due to space – particularly in terms of outside space – that other schools might not have. On the other hand, the businesses and companies that live and work alongside our school provide us with unique opportunities.

Our physical environment

Because our school is housed inside a (admittedly very nice, very new) tower block, it is quite a unique environment. These are a few of the features that we think contribute to our particular brand of belonging.

- We want our children to feel that the entire school is for them. Our **staff room** is at the heart of the school and it has glass walls. It can be anxiety inducing for some children to knock on a staff room door when they need to speak to a particular adult – this way our children can see if their teacher is inside and can signal to them that they would like to speak to them without any uncertainty.
- Where possible, our corridors have **curved walls**, which make it easier for those who are partially sighted to navigate the space by touch. This was a very deliberate design feature from the get-go: we try to anticipate future needs where we can.
- For an increasing number of our children, full-time learning in mainstream classrooms is challenging. We have thought carefully about how our corridors and other spaces (such as therapy and soft-play rooms) can be made to feel like **an extension of the learning environment** through the information available on displays.
- Because our **outdoor space** is limited, we do not have separate EYFS, KS1 and KS2 playgrounds. While we thought this was a challenge at first, it has actually had a really lovely consequence. Many of our older pupils, who in other contexts might think themselves 'too mature' for some of the play equipment, continue to regularly access messy play and a number of the outdoor games usually used by younger children.

Bringing parents into the school

As mentioned previously, we want our pupils to not feel excluded from the affluence and innovation that is so evident in our local community – and that's really important for parents too. We want them to feel that they belong here.

When the school was first opened, and we only had a couple of year groups in the building, parents would drop their child at their classroom in the morning. Unfortunately, now that we have 500 children in the building, we simply do not have the space for parents to do this so now they have to drop their child at reception. We knew from speaking to our parents that they really missed seeing their child to their class, and so we've tried to come up with other ways of making parents feel included.

Family Fridays

Every second Friday of a half term, each year group has a family training.

- Parents arrive at 9am with their child and head to our hall.
- Breakfast is provided, which we all eat together.
- In the hall both adult and child receive 20 minutes of training together.
- The training events offer an opportunity for parents to practise supporting learning (for example phonics) with their child, with staff on hand to help.
- The parents leave afterwards with a bag of resources that they can use to support learning at home.

Parents know at the start of the academic year which Fridays their child will be having training and generally they are really well attended.

Learning presentations

At the end of every unit of work, we will have a learning presentation that parents are invited to attend. These are always oracy-based – sometimes through debates, for example – which provide an opportunity for children to re-cap and re-embed their learning and for parents to hear about what we have been working on.

Parent coffee mornings with SLT

These are held once a half term. They are very informal, with no set agenda, so that what is discussed is genuinely shaped by the parents and not about the school giving updates. It's an opportunity to ask questions and raise any issues in an informal and relaxed setting.

Belonging within King's Cross estate

Some new commercial estates – like King's Cross – can lack a sense of warmth and community, so we try to be proactive and do our bit to generate a sense of togetherness in our area. Through doing this, we've been able to secure some really rich and rewarding opportunities for our children.

- We do PE on a MUGA (Multi-Use Games Area) in the commercial building opposite, which also functions as our second playground.
- Our **art show** is hosted every year at Central St Martin's College of Art: these are exhibitions that our parents, and the public, attend.
- We take our children to every exhibition at **Lightroom**, which is a modern art gallery around the corner from our school.
- We take our children to the nearby **Waitrose** where we can bring their financial education to life in a real-world context. Waitrose have also donated refreshments for our carol services in the past.

We adopt a 'don't ask, don't get' approach when it comes to working with the local businesses across the King's Cross estate. We do have to invest leadership time into doing this, but we believe it's worth it for the sense of community and togetherness that it generates. By the end of their time with us at KCA, our children generally feel at home in this part of London.

Lessons we have learned

- If you want every child to feel known, you must **build routines that force you to talk about every child regularly** – otherwise some will quietly slip through the gaps.
- If you remove financial and logistical barriers, participation rises dramatically. Belonging grows fastest when **opportunity is universal, not optional**. Prioritise decisions that make this happen.
- If you create **clear communication channels and agreed protocols** with parents from the outset, difficult conversations become manageable rather than combustible.

Time to think

Questions for reflecting on your current setting	Questions to consider for further action
• What processes exist in your setting that enable school leaders to build a holistic picture of individual learners? • List all the ways that the statement 'children and young people are celebrated for who they are' is demonstrated in your setting. • What systems and structures are in place to support positive parent–school relations in your setting? Where is your strongest practice? How do you know?	• Reflect on your catchment area. Do the majority of children live nearby? What differences are there between where most students live and where your school is situated? What actions could you take to resolve any potential dissonance being experienced? • What processes or elements of school life could be improved by having greater clarity or transparency? What conversations do you find yourself repeating? What could improve that? • In your area, where are the opportunities for learning or for sharing students' work?
Your commitment for further reflection and action 1. 2. 3.	

Deeside Sixth Form, Flintshire

Miriam Riddell, Headteacher

About us and our community

Deeside 6th (D6th) is a purpose-built sixth form college that opened in 2016. We are part of Coleg Cambria – a large Further and Higher Education provider in North Wales, with over 7000 full-time students across five sites. At D6th we have around 600 students on roll and all learners study three A-levels, plus the Advanced Skills Baccalaureate Wales (ASBW) to complement their academic studies. While there is a lot of choice in Flintshire when it comes to A-level study (with many local schools offering them), we are the only sixth form college in the area.

Because of Flintshire's border with Cheshire, we recruit students from both Wales and England. Our learners from England often choose to study in Wales due to the flexibility of the AS/A2 model (which Wales retained when England returned to the linear model). Our students join us from over twenty different high schools, from a wide catchment that spans the Wirral to Rhyl. Because of that, very few of our students live in the immediate locality, and so we work hard to generate a sense of community and togetherness within our site.

What belonging means to us

D6th had only been open for three years when I became Head in 2019, and so I have been privileged to be able to help shape the vision and values as the sixth form established itself in the community. In order for someone to feel a sense of belonging in a place, they need to understand the values that are lived there: so for us, belonging begins with people understanding what we're about from the moment they walk in.

When you're a sixth form college, the majority of students are only with you for two years. And so while there is a focus on welcoming students when they join us, we cannot help but also be even more focused on their futures and next steps. Whether students go on to university, higher apprenticeships and training, or employment, we want to clearly communicate that our college is going to help them make that transition and so we are intentional about making sure we feel 'different' to school. Often students choose a college over a secondary school sixth form because they want a fresh start and the opportunity to rebrand. It's important to us that our college feels like a safe and inclusive place for students to do that, while also encouraging them to be their authentic selves.

Part of what we're about is also making sure that you know you're in Wales when you come through our doors. We aim to promote and celebrate our Welsh culture in a way that includes those students and staff who join us from across the border. This is conveyed partly through visuals – flags and bilingual posters/displays – as well as incidental Welsh in classrooms and the option for all learners to access exam papers and ASBW lessons in Welsh. For students joining us from England (or those who are not Welsh-speaking), we have introductory Welsh phrases in our student handbook.

Relations

Relationships are absolutely crucial for us. We want to challenge the assumption that colleges are large and impersonal, allowing students to fly under the radar. Because students are not with us for long, we need to prioritise getting to know them (and letting them get to know us) from the outset. These are some of the things we do that help us quickly build strong relationships with our students.

D6th Connection programme

In May 2025, the Research Commission on Engagement and Lead Indicators (RCELI) published a study on how pupil engagement changed across academic Year 2024/25. It made evident that pupils' average enjoyment of school falls as they move through the key stages. Almost every country with available data sees this decline, but the report noted that this was more pronounced in England, 'suggesting that disengagement is not just a symptom of age, but something atypical happening in our context.' One suggested reason for this was a loss of belonging as they move through the key stages (ImpactEd Group, 2025).

As a secondary school teacher, I had always tried to bring a little of what felt familiar and warm about primary school into my practice. In some ways, teaching A-level is more similar to primary teaching than key stages 3 and 4: we see the same classes for long periods of time each week, enabling us to build up rapport quickly when the conditions are right. Through my experience as a governor of a primary school, I saw that all of the care and attention that regularly goes into transition between key stage 2 and key stage 3 was not being replicated for progression into sixth form. It baffled me that we were expecting learners to transfer from high school into a new setting like college without that same level of support.

So, we devised the Connection programme, which is based around four strands: transition, induction, enrichment and a two-year progression plan.

Transition

This aims to replicate for Year 11 students some of the common support for KS2 to KS3 transition.

- We deliver personalised **assemblies** in our feeder schools. These are delivered by myself and some core staff at D6th, as well as alumni students from each school.
- We use these assemblies, and our ongoing collaboration with each feeder school, to design bespoke **follow-up sessions based on identified needs**. For example, there are GCSE masterclasses to support attainment, as well as A-level taster lessons in subjects that would be new to many students such as psychology, law and film studies.
- We offer **summer activities** for students to participate in and make new connections, such as sporting events and film clubs.
- We use our **student ambassadors** from the first year to act as mentors for applicants to our college so they have a reassuring peer to reach out to if they have questions or are feeling overwhelmed.

Induction

We carefully analyse the schools that students are coming from so that we can **identify those who are joining us on their own** or with only one or two peers. These students are placed in induction groups together to avoid them feeling like an outsider to already-established friendship groups. We do the same for learners with certain additional learning needs who may need to be more closely supported on their first day. We use festival-style coloured wristbands to organise the groups, which works well.

The **induction activities** are spread over two days, with day one focusing largely on operational activities (getting onto the Wi-Fi, exploring the building) and day two focused on A-level tasters, providing a final opportunity to try out subjects before committing to their chosen three.

We also ensure that **A2 Subject Ambassadors** support each induction group to help facilitate friendships and support with any issues that arise during the two days.

In our **welcome assembly** for new students, every single adult who works in the building introduces themselves to the new cohort: the teachers and support staff, but also the cleaners, canteen staff, estates teams and student services.

Enrichment

We are proud of our enrichment offer, and we run a freshers' fayre in the first week to give students the opportunity to sign up to clubs and events. Engagement with the extra-curricular offer is something that we regularly track as part of our ongoing relationship building with students: we want to know what they are interested in beyond their studies.

We run a Festival of Futures event every year at the end of Year 12. The festival spans three weeks and includes every subject department putting on trips, university visits, guest speakers and events to showcase different related careers. Students compile their experiences and insights into a booklet which then forms part of their UCAS applications the following autumn term.

Two-year progression plan

Our two-year progression plan is two-fold. Firstly, it is designed to help students connect with their subjects and home in on how they want to take them forward (including potentially into a career). Secondly, it enables them to develop important transferable skills for future employment or study.

There is an emphasis on the behaviours, skills and dispositions that will lead to long-term success such as resilience and determination. The emphasis on how subjects link to careers and skills has positively impacted on retention and progression from AS to A2, with over 90%

of our students now returning for their second year (this had dropped to around 78% in the years immediately following the pandemic).

Progress coaches

In 2019, we piloted a move away from tutor-based pastoral support to a progress coach model. Progress coaches are non-teaching members of staff, and we believed that moving to this model would have two main benefits.

1. Subject teachers would be able to solely focus on the delivery of their curricula and courses.
2. Students would have a dedicated coaching team who would be on hand to support throughout the day, allowing for more immediate and flexible support.

We have three progress coaches, each responsible for just under 200 tutees each. Our progress coaches support our learners in a number of ways.

- They deliver **weekly sessions** to their coaching group that both cover the mandatory pastoral curriculum as well as responding to key issues going on in the world (for example, sessions on positive and progressive masculinity).
- Coaches have an active role in **tracking attainment** as well as guiding learners through their UCAS, degree apprenticeship or employment applications.
- They are a crucial **intermediary between student, parent and college**. They meet regularly with the senior leadership team, support services, SENDCo, and academic skills facilitator. They are ideally positioned to ensure that our learners are always being considered holistically.

In order to make the progress coach team as effective as possible, we moved their office right to the centre of the building. It has enabled the pastoral care and support we provide to become the beating heart of the building. As Head, I spend time working in the PC office every day, which helps me stay grounded in the daily experiences of our learners.

One really nice qualitative measure of the impact our progress coaches have is the fact that so many of our alumni keep in touch with them when they move on. Former students can often be found coming back to deliver workshops (for example, on writing personal statements, or interview techniques) and sharing good luck videos with the current students during exam periods.

Since we implemented this model, our attendance and retention rates have been improving year on year. We are convinced that the relationships between progress coaches and their coachees has contributed significantly to that.

Agency

A big part of belonging for us is ensuring that our staff and students feel that they are active participants in college life, and also that they feel trusted and valued by us.

The gift of time

For students

One of the challenges of education at key stage 5 is helping students develop their independent study skills, especially as most are encountering 'free periods' for the first time. Like many sixth forms, we felt that students were not necessarily making effective use of their non-directed time. We had also noticed that attendance had dipped after Covid, especially on days when students only had one or two lessons. We knew that a lot of our students had jobs outside of college, and at least a few of them were choosing to work a shift on days with low contact time rather than coming into college for a couple of hours of teaching.

One major change we implemented a few years ago was to move to a **four-day week** for students. Each learner has one day to work from home each week (which day that is depends on their subject blocks). They still have their full five hours a week in each subject, but it reduces the number of free/study periods that they have on site. We also keep Wednesday afternoons free of lessons (similar to universities) so that learners have time within the week to complete work-related experience and enrichment. Many of our students are bussed into college and so do not have a lot of flexibility in terms of what time they arrive and leave each day, so we wanted to make sure this was built into the timetable.

Our students have responded really positively to this change. They do not need to tell us what work they are doing on their day from home, although they will often discuss this with their progress coach. We deliver mandatory study skills sessions as part of induction, and independent study is regularly revisited as part of the programme delivered by our progress coaches. Our outcomes have improved year on year since introducing this change, and students appreciate and value the trust we place in them.

For staff

It's also important to us to give staff the gift of time. Because we do not timetable lessons on Wednesday afternoons, all staff can work from home then (if they wish) and can catch up on PPA tasks.

We also changed the meeting structure so that we have one staff meeting slot after lunch on a Monday, which means that staff are not required to stay late throughout the week. Our philosophy is only to meet if we need to, keep regular meetings to a minimum and aim to keep all meetings to a maximum of thirty minutes. In weeks when we do not have meetings, this gives staff an extra hour to see learners outside of lesson times for one-to-ones.

Legacy and contribution

We want our students to feel that they are actively contributing to our college, and that we value those contributions. As well as encouraging students to take on leadership and responsibility within the college, we try to capitalise on students' experiences by helping them share their insight and experience with their peers and those who will attend D6th after them.

Subject ambassadors

We run a successful subject ambassador programme that involves learners supporting subject areas at events like open evenings, mentoring new students as part of induction and offering peer tutoring services. Any student can book a one-to-one session with a subject ambassador using a Google form that we co-ordinate.

6th *Sense* magazine

Our students self-publish a literary and cultural magazine called *6th Sense* three times a year. The magazine is written, curated, edited and designed by students and includes a wide variety of articles such as literary criticism, film and music reviews, opinion pieces on current affairs, and revision and learning tips.

Pupil parliament

Cambria as a college is very keen to ensure student voice and engagement is at the heart of every decision we make. This involves not just having a student rep body across all sites, but also having students involved in staff recruitment interviews, the college self-evaluation cycle, subject annual surveys and also site-specific student voice programmes such as our own D6th pupil parliament. Our pupil parliament enables our students to shape what we do at D6th and provides data for us to make operational decisions with them in mind. We use simple Google forms and our custom *Cambria* app (where they can view their timetable, report sickness, track assignment deadlines and access up-to-date college news) to stay on the pulse of what our learners need.

D6th Legacy

This year, the progress coaches team have compiled a *D6th Legacy* book along with some of our alumni students, which is a magazine filled with guidance, advice, anecdotes and kind words from past students that is shared with our new learners to help settle them in and introduce them to the college.

Staff practice

We empower staff to share good practice by separating teaching and learning strategies from ordinary staff meetings. This means we have dedicated time once a half term where staff chair their own meeting and take turns to showcase strategies that are working well in their areas. This helps our team stay innovative. We are big believers in the benefit of sharing across subject disciplines and so there is also a 'peer observation' programme that staff can sign up to if they want to observe, and learn from, the practice of someone in a different faculty.

Space and place

We are very lucky to have a lovely, ergonomic building that has been carefully designed for us. But we know that building belonging is about much more than what a space looks like: it's about how it is inhabited and lived in. We try to foster a sense of openness, professionalism and autonomy in our spaces.

Open, productive and professional spaces

We want our students to be comfortable in our building, and we do have a relaxed and friendly atmosphere, but we also want to use the physical environment to encourage the sorts of independent, self-regulatory behaviours that will help students be successful.

Rather than a reception, we have a **student services area** in our entrance foyer, which is a hub for supporting students with a variety of things such as transport, finance, sexual health and daily operational issues. We felt that this more accurately reflected the support hubs available at universities and in workplaces.

Instead of a common room, we have a **number of open-plan co-working areas** throughout the college. So there's a lot of choice about where students can work and socialise, but they are always visible to the staff around the building – having no dark corners or places to hide helps students regulate their behaviour. Similarly, all the communal areas – with the exception of our main atrium – are furnished with chairs and tables, rather than the sofas that were there previously.

The vast majority of our classrooms have large internal windows, and we always teach with classroom doors open. This means that teaching staff can monitor the shared spaces, but more importantly it contributes to the culture of openness and collaboration that we try to foster at D6th.

We regularly do one-to-one feedback with students, often outside of the classroom. Our corridors feature ergonomically designed sloping ledges that are ideal for resting a laptop, tablet or notes on – almost like a shared lectern. This simple addition to the physical environment helps these conversations feel natural, productive and purposeful. You'll regularly see staff and students in conversation in the corridors. Because it happens so often, and the environment supports it, there is never any assumption that a corridor conversation is about anything other than learning.

Come as you are: Space for authenticity and self-expression

As previously mentioned, many students relish the rebranding opportunity that a fresh start at college can afford them. Like many colleges, we do not have a uniform policy and students are free to attend in whatever clothing they are comfortable in – giving them the space to express themselves. Staff are also welcome to dress more casually if they prefer and are encouraged to show up to work as their authentic selves. Students refer to staff by their first names, which helps cultivate mutual respect as well as pre-empting university and workplace environments.

This self-expression extends into our learning environments. We are fortunate to have a large site with plenty of space, and so most staff have a designated classroom that is not shared with other teachers. Staff are welcome (and encouraged) to personalise the environment, with displays reflecting personal aesthetics and interests. This helps keep learning personal and grounded.

Some staff have taken this a step further into digital spaces, where we know our students are spending increasing amounts of time. Some have active presences on Instagram, regularly sharing not only student work and displays, but also content directly related to learning – these accounts are followed by staff and students. One colleague has set up a TikTok account where he posts educational – and funny! – videos for students, helping them explore different aspects of their law studies. The crucial thing is that this is not a requirement of staff, and it works because it is based on genuine interest, enthusiasm and connection with students.

Lessons we have learned

- Establishing the **culture** you want starts and ends with you as a leader.
- Being **visible**, especially at the start and end of the day, is crucial for staying connected to what is going on.
- **Collaboration** is crucial: working with staff to allow everyone to play to their strengths.

Time to think

Questions for reflecting on your current setting	Questions to consider for further action
• Reflect on your transition processes both into and out of your setting. What messages about belonging are encoded into that practice? Who are students introduced to? • If you are a school leader, where do you work during the day? How easy or difficult is it for you to tap into the daily life of your setting? • How do you demonstrate to students and staff that their time is valued?	• Does your physical environment encourage the sorts of behaviour you want to instil in your students? What adaptations could be made to improve this? • How much of your wider enrichment offer is accessible during the school day? Which students might be unable to access after-school clubs? • Are there opportunities to strengthen the conversation between academic and pastoral staff, to help provide a more rounded, holistic picture of students?
Your commitment for further reflection and action 1. 2. 3.	

Time to think: Checking our assumptions

School leaders and teachers demonstrate tremendous amounts of empathy daily, many going above and beyond to anticipate the needs of learners, colleagues and community members. But psychology teaches us that there may be some instances where we don't actually know what we think we know – and that acting on these false assumptions can erode belonging.

The Fundamental Attribution Error

According to psychologist Geoffrey Cohen, the Fundamental Attribution Error (FAE) is 'one of the most widespread and least appreciated "psychological sins," which wreaks havoc on belonging' (Cohen, 2022).

FAE is a common cognitive bias where we place undue emphasis on personality-based explanations for behaviour and under-emphasise situational factors. So someone who pushes in front of you in a queue is a 'fundamentally selfish person', and not someone who is distracted by hearing bad news and failed to notice you standing there first. Or, this student didn't do their homework because they are 'lazy', and not because they were busy caring for a sibling.

Making the Fundamental Attribution Error is natural and we all do it, but we need to be aware of it. Research suggests that we can try to combat this tendency by:

- Probing our conclusions with questions that ask 'why **else** could they have acted in that way?'
- Training ourselves to adopt the 'perspective of a neutral third party who wants the best for all involved' (Kross, 2021).

- Taking a step back and performing a **values affirmation**. Reminding ourselves of what our values are helps us connect with our better nature, curbing our defensive need to blame others (Cohen, 2022).

Can you recall examples where you may have made a Fundamental Attribution Error? It might have been with a student, a colleague, or a community member.

- What else might have explained their behaviour?
- What processes or approaches might help you to be more mindful of situational influences?
- Could there be a benefit to developing a shared language with staff where you can challenge FAE?

Thinking like a scientist

We can also help overcome FAE by developing what Adam Grant calls the ability to 'think like a scientist' – holding our beliefs lightly, testing them and being willing to revise them in light of new evidence. In our settings, this can help us treat our interpretations of behaviour not as a fixed truth but as a hypothesis to be further explored. When we assume we know why someone has acted a certain way, we close down curiosity. When we remain open to being wrong, we create space for understanding (Grant, 2021).

Perspective mistaking

Another mistake we can all make is when we try to put ourselves in the position of others. Behavioural scientist Nicholas Epley suggests that we are not as good at doing this as we might think, and that trying to take someone else's perspective can actually make us less perceptive (Epley, 2014). In part this is because of a very obvious mistake that most of us make: we put ourselves into their position, failing to account for the fact that the person in question is **not us**.

Epley's suggestion for overcoming this is to shift our attempts from perspective-**taking** to perspective-**getting**. And the best way to get someone's perspective? Ask them.

What perspectives have you taken recently? Are there opportunities for you to get those perspectives, to check for any assumptions that you may have made?

It may also be worth considering how you could introduce some of these concepts in age-appropriate ways to students, to help them in their own interactions.

Examples in practice

- Bantock Primary School adopt a culture of curiosity as leaders where they prioritise understanding over action, an example being their approach to strengthening their relationship with their Gypsy, Roma and Traveller families (page 29).
- When students' behaviour is not meeting expectations, there is a high risk for making the Fundamental Attribution Error. Many schools have processes and strategies in place to ensure that students are supported to share their perspectives in psychological safety – for example, through reparation conversations at Saracens High School (page 7) and Ferndown Upper School (page 111), or through emotion coaching at Flakefleet Primary School (page 15).
- An important part of getting perspective, rather than taking it, involves relinquishing some control over the agenda. At King's Cross Academy, their parent coffee mornings (page 55) avoid school-determined agenda items and updates and instead are an open forum for parents to give feedback, share ideas and ask the questions that matter to them.

Acklam Grange School, Middlesbrough

Lucy Gowland, Deputy Headteacher

About us and our community

Our school is a large and popular 11–16 academy in Middlesbrough, a central pillar of our local community and part of a growing multi-academy trust (The Legacy Learning Trust). We serve a vast and diverse catchment area, from some of the highest areas of social need nationally to more affluent suburbs.

A community is much more than data and metrics, but nevertheless our data does signal a stark reality: some of our students live in the lowest 2% of IDACI (Income Deprivation Affecting Children Index) defined communities, with a significant proportion living in the bottom 1%. We are attuned to how the lived experiences of our young people, regardless of their economic status, can impact on how they show up to school. It's our job to meet them where they are.

At the heart of our identity at AGS is the belief that 'Mighty oaks from little acorns grow.' It is central to our logo and inseparable from our culture. We aim to provide a steady ground and nurturing climate that affords every student the chance to grow deeply, stand tall and flourish. That's why we place belonging, safety and care at our core.

What belonging means to us

Middlesbrough, like some other parts of the UK, does not always get the best press. Persistent negative headlines can lead to individuals and communities developing low self-esteem and low self-efficacy. We want to flip that narrative: our aim is for our young people to be filled with confidence and self-worth, and to be proud of where they come from.

To do this, they need to know that we care about them as individuals. Our 'One Curriculum Commitment' combines our challenging academic curriculum with social, moral, cultural and character education – development of the whole child is not a bolt-on or addition to the curriculum, it **is** the curriculum. We explicitly talk about the AGS family – and it is the responsibility of every adult within our family to help our young people develop. Every interaction inside and outside the classroom shapes and moulds them. We believe every single student has a talent and it is our shared responsibility to help them discover, develop and grow those talents.

Belonging, for us, is not the soft option: we view it as the necessary and crucial foundation for everything we do. Quality teaching and academic achievement are, of course, hugely important and we invest heavily in providing the best possible learning experience for our young people, but they can only make the best of that when they feel safe and ready to learn. By prioritising this emotional safety and secure attachment that belonging provides we consistently see our young people break glass ceilings, achieving much more than data, their prior learning, their families or even they themselves ever believed possible.

Agency

Particularly given some of the narratives perpetuated about our town in the press, it's vital that our young people understand their worth and the power they have to influence their lives and the lives of others. We know that often fear of failure can limit individuals' sense of agency. To combat this, we try to help students understand errors and mistakes as a normal part of the learning journey and reframe them as opportunities for deeper learning and growth. At AGS, we talk about wanting our young people to be the driver of their educational journey, not just a passenger.

AGS PRIDE: our blueprint for building agency

We use our school values – known as AGS PRIDE – to help students (and staff) build their sense of self-worth and self-efficacy. Loosely inspired by PiXL's LORIC attributes (leadership, organisation, resilience, initiative and communication), the choice of 'pride' was intentional: we want our young people to be proud to be from Middlesbrough, to be part of the AGS family and, most importantly, to be authentically themselves.

The table below demonstrates how we translate those values into practice, helping us to cultivate agency in every corner of the school building.

PRIDE value	The call to agency	What it looks like in practice
Perseverance	Be fearless, embrace challenge and do not give up!	Grit: Redefining struggle as growth, not failure.
Respect	Treat everyone with care, courtesy and consideration.	Empathy: Creating a secure social environment where diverse voices can be heard.
Initiative	Be independent, pave your own future. What are you waiting for?	Ownership: Encouraging self-starting, critical thinking and proactive problem-solving.
Direction	Use your aspirations to inspire others and lead the way.	Vision: Connecting today's effort to future goals and inspiring collective achievement.
Expression	Use your imagination and communicate clearly.	Voice: Empowering students to share their authentic thoughts and creative ideas.

PRIDE values

These five values are woven into the fabric of our culture and underpin everything we do. They are regularly revisited in Let's Get Going (tutorial) and PRIDE lessons (RSHE) and are a golden thread throughout the school day. They are important to us, and our students, because we believe they are the values and skills that will enable them to make a difference for themselves, their families and their communities in the future.

Our reward systems are built around the PRIDE values, with staff praising work, attitude and behaviours that exemplify growth in each area. For example, a pupil may be awarded a Perseverance point for using the 'dot don't stop' strategy (designed to overcome perfectionism and writer's block) to push on and extend an answer in a lesson; a Year Leader might issue an end of term award for a pupil who has excelled in an extracurricular activity; or the headteacher might invite a group of pupils to share hot chocolate and celebrate the respect they showed when supporting a local resident in the community.

Headspace for learning

For young people to meet the high aspirations we have for them, we needed to make sure they had the skills to be present and ready to work in school. After the pandemic, like many schools, we saw more students struggling to regulate as they readjusted from periods of at-home learning.

Our **headspace for learning** strategy was developed to help bring clarity to students and staff about what they can do during moments of stress, overwhelm or dysregulation. The strategy includes three avenues that staff and students can follow that are clearly understood across our school. When we introduced these strategies, we taught students about the underpinning neuroscience so that they understood how each option could help them.

- **Share It**: Students are encouraged to share concerns with a trusted adult or peer.
- **Shelve It**: This is not about undermining or invalidating what students are experiencing, but is about acknowledging the feelings and placing them on a shelf (to be returned to) so that learning can recommence. This was the strategy that needed the most careful introduction so that children felt affirmed and supported. It is underpinned by our **Mindful Five** practices, which include discrete breathing techniques that students (and staff!) regularly use to help ground themselves and return their attention to learning.
- **Space For It**: This acknowledges that, in some situations, students need to temporarily remove themselves from the classroom (remaining within the teacher's eyeline through windows/glass panels on doors).

The language staff use is consistent and aligned with the strategy. When staff notice that a student is dysregulated, they will prompt them with phrases such as 'Would you like to **share it**?', 'Do you feel able to **shelve it** for this lesson?', 'Do you need **space for it**?' This helps students feel seen and gives them a sense of control over how they are feeling. It helps them be present and self-aware, without fear of judgement.

Cultivating intrinsic drive

In any school, there will always be a functional need for rewards and consequences to celebrate the positives and challenge the negatives. However, our core belief is that intrinsic motivation – rather than extrinsic compliance – is the ultimate engine of resilience. We don't want to train students to follow rules; we want to instil in them the self-governance to make the right choices for themselves.

When it comes to praise, we focus on:

- Effort over outcome.
- Character over compliance.
- Self-worth over external validation.

PRIDE Pod

Our PRIDE Pod is perhaps the best expression of where this approach has led us. Every few weeks or so, a member of our SLT sets up camp in a different part of the school building, which is usually led by invitation from a faculty or extra-curricular lead. PRIDE Pod is a voluntary, open invitation for students to share work that they are proud of. They will discuss the work, having meaningful conversations about what *they* did that has led to them wanting to share the work.

This gives students the opportunity to reflect on their progress and judge themselves against their own expectations. Every student attending the Pod will be celebrated: it's not about hitting a certain standard, it's about students recognising and affirming their own achievements and progress. Because PRIDE Pod is voluntary, we are also able to identify students who perhaps are not feeling as positive about their learning or progress and our staff can then make concerted efforts in their interactions with those students to build up that confidence and self-worth.

Showing up authentically: Pupil G

Pupil G joined us as a founder member of our Oakland Hub - our additionally-resourced provision. His ASD (autistic spectrum disorder) meant that the world felt very loud and unpredictable and, on joining us, his family was not sure that mainstream school would be possible.

Since joining us, Pupil G has become a beloved member of our school community. He didn't just find his place with us, he found a vocation as our self-appointed 'Chief Seagull Scarer', a role that still sees him running through our courtyard with his slope board and flat cap, emitting seagull calls (genuinely more realistic than the creatures themselves). In some environments, this might leave Pupil G open to dismissal or rejection by his peers. Not at AGS: here, he is a legend. His growth was palpable when he applied for, interviewed for and was appointed as Deputy Head Student of Acklam Grange.

A powerful illustration of G's journey can be seen in these extracts of emails from his parents, sent throughout his school career.

- **Transition between Year 6 and Year 7**: 'G is displaying signs of high anxiety … he cries every day and he is adamant that he won't go [to school] and I can't make him.'
- **In Year 9**: 'His sense of self-worth, emotional regulation and academic abilities have sky-rocketed at AGS. Teaching assistants and teachers

have a high level of understanding of Autism Spectrum Condition and accommodate G's needs involving him in decisions within the school setting.'

- **In Year 11**: 'Thank you for the difference you make every day and for continuing to inspire G to feel valued and connected.'

Relations

While we believe that relationships have always been at the heart of AGS, we have been on a journey over the last ten years or so to further strengthen connections at all levels.

Simple and clear expectations

In an SLT meeting, our headteacher challenged us to list every school rule from memory. After 30 minutes of scribbling, the truth was undeniable: we couldn't recall them all. And if we couldn't remember them, how could we expect the students to live by them?

This experience led us to look again at our rules and try to isolate key themes. In the end, we broke down a myriad of complex regulations into three simple rules:

- Respect yourself.
- Respect each other.
- Respect the community.

We have found that every behaviour, positive or negative, fits under these three banners. And the language shift has been transformative. Conversations that we have about conduct have not only become more positive and relational, but we've also shifted away from bureaucratic or administrative issues to talking about underlying values. 'Don't litter, please' becomes 'Have you thought about how that litter affects our community?'

Small things that make a big difference

Following relational practice training, we confirmed our mission to Build, Maintain and Repair relationships across the school. This was operationalised as **four small things**: specific staff behaviours designed to make a big difference (originally this was three small things – we added the fourth after lockdown).

- **Meet and greet**: Making sure children feel seen through warm greetings every day and at the start of every lesson, ideally with a smile, eye contact and use of the child's name.
- **PIP and RIP (Praise in Public, Reprimand in Private)**: Recognising that what we pay attention to is what we get more of, we use positive reinforcement to celebrate success while maintaining dignity through private, firm and warm redirection.
- **Deliberate language**: When speaking to students following an incident, moving away from asking 'why?' (which triggers the defensive limbic brain) to asking 'what happened?' This co-regulation strategy allows pupils to be heard and enables them to regulate before they reflect.
- **Talking about experiences**: Recognising that, upon returning from lockdown, our pupils were increasingly likely to share difficult emotions, experiences and possible disclosures, we further equipped staff with the skills to listen, empathise and support.

We value these low-effort, high-impact tools, accessible to all staff. We have also taken the opportunity over the years to deepen our understanding of relational practice. For example, through our partnership with Middlesbrough's Virtual Headteacher and Educational Psychology Service we have been a pilot school for the PROCLAIM Project (Providing Rich Opportunities for Children who are Looked After In and around Middlesbrough) (Banks and Garforth, 2022). This partnership has further up-skilled our staff as trauma-responsive educational neuroscientists.

Taught, not caught

In a community as wonderfully diverse as ours, we cannot leave social conduct to chance. For a number of students, the stability of rules, routines and familiar structures only exists within our walls. We don't 'expect' good behaviour: we explicitly teach and model it. We recognise that staff are the primary architects of our culture, and we are grateful for their buy-in and commitment to creating a calm, supportive and consistent learning environment for our young people.

We believe that conduct, and therefore culture, needs to be taught, not caught. As part of our One Curriculum Commitment, we explicitly cover behaviour, conduct and values as part of our PRIDE curriculum, assemblies and our **Let's Get Going** tutor sessions. Pupils receive daily explicit teaching about the behaviours our family expects and why.

Systems that support

It was important that our person-centred approaches were underpinned by robust systems to support our day-to-day practice.

- Our **Key Student Index** serves as a live intelligence tool, providing staff with the essential context they need in order to tailor their interactions with pupils (e.g. so they are aware of specific triggers for children experiencing trauma).
- Our **ARC forums** (Achievement, Reintegration and Care) are fortnightly, year-group-focused meetings that provide a structured space for staff to synchronise support, ensuring that academic and pastoral conversations are not being siloed.

Resetting relationships: Pupil A

On their first day with us, Pupil A bypassed their key worker, walked straight towards the headteacher and – in no uncertain terms – told him where he could go. Pupil A lived in an area of high social deprivation, speaks English as an additional language and has an ASD diagnosis. We recognised his behaviour on day one as a test of his boundaries and proof that we did not yet have his trust.

As staff, we refused to be triggered by his distress. Instead, we applied the PACE model (Playfulness, Acceptance, Curiosity, Empathy) – meeting every interaction with calm, curious interest. Through this, and over time, we identified his specific triggers. He often experienced sensory overwhelm in the dining room. In addition, his limited diet was creating barriers to social integration. Our Whole School Behaviour Manager arranged a Teesside Tapas spread: a low-stakes, playful way of inviting co-regulation in an ordinarily high-stress situation.

Space and place

Hopefully by now it is clear that a large focus of our work is on instilling a sense of pride and confidence in our children and young people. This is something that we try to reflect and communicate through our physical environment too.

Demonstrating PRIDE in our community

As part of our ongoing commitment to cultivating pride in our students, we try to use the physical environment – as well as whole-school events – to instil pupils with self-belief and remind them of our pride in them.

Visual cues around school

- Our school building is situated quite far back from the road, which means we have an extensive walkway to the school building. We have large PRIDE banners that flank the entryway, reminding students and staff every day as they enter the building of our values.
- Our shared courtyard (in the heart of the school) includes designated areas for reflection and mindfulness, including reminders for some of our **Mindful Five** strategies: **FOFBOC stations** (Feet on Floor, Bum on Chair) are designated areas for quiet self-regulation, as well as designated routes for students to follow if they would prefer a walking mindfulness practice, such as **Samurai Walk routes**.
- The location of PRIDE Pod changes every time, ensuring regular opportunities to shine a spotlight on different parts of the school building. (This is also a great way to keep all our staff involved.)
- Our large dining area has been intentionally decorated with murals and artwork that reflect the local community and the wider world. We wanted to communicate to students both that where they live is important, and that the whole world is out there for them to explore.

Culture Day

Culture Day 2025 was the culmination of a year-long, pupil-led project to celebrate the 50+ home languages spoken by our community and the diverse backgrounds that contribute to our school community.

Designed to be a 'festival of identity', our courtyard was decorated, including a grand floral archway and a centre stage. Students attended dressed in clothing that represented their culture. The day was filled with celebration, curiosity and learning. It was a clear visual display of the fact that, while we are all different and have unique perspectives, we all belong at AGS.

A place for shared experiences

As well as being places of pride and celebration, often schools represent one of the few shared spaces where children can experience and navigate difficult feelings together and in safety. As a school, we don't shy away from our responsibility to help them do this.

Community Wall of Remembrance

Our Community Wall of Remembrance is a permanent tribute comprised of over 3000 hand-crafted poppies – one for every soldier from Middlesbrough who fell during the Great War. Each poppy was carefully researched, transforming a list of casualties into individual stories of humanity (and very much aligning with the importance we place on respecting our community – past, present and future).

The Wall of Remembrance is the focal point for our annual Remembrance Service, which is now attended by nearly 2000 people, plus many more who requested to join via live-stream.

Navigating grief

We talk about being a family at AGS. Families are not only there to celebrate the good together: they also mourn together. In 2022, we very suddenly lost a cherished member of our staff family. We were faced with the challenge of how we honour their life while also protecting the emotional wellbeing of our young people.

We made the decision to welcome the funeral procession through the school grounds. We formed a (non-compulsory) guard of honour as our treasured AGS family member passed along the oval route of our car park. It was an extremely emotional day for all of us, but it was also an incredible display of togetherness; and it meant a lot to us that the family and friends of that staff member welcomed the school's involvement and our desire to say goodbye as a community.

A place you choose to be

For us, belonging is evidenced in the many former pupils who return to AGS to work, the alumni who regularly return to share their journeys with us and the scores of staff – including the current Head and Deputy – who choose Acklam Grange for their own children. This isn't just loyalty; it's a testament to a community that people choose to be a part of.

Lessons we have learned

- **Safety before syllabus.** Brains that are in survival mode cannot learn. We need to prioritise students feeling safe and seen.
- **Language has to be backed up by action.** If we talk about the AGS family, we have to back that up with tangible evidence and everyday practice.

- **Mighty oaks from little acorns grow**. While some of our systems and approaches have grown and developed over the years, we have to start with small and simple acorns – and give them time to grow. They **will** leave a legacy.

Time to think

Questions for reflecting on your current setting	Questions to consider for further action
• What beliefs are held within/about your local community that may be impacting on the sense of belonging felt by students, staff and parents? • What beliefs are at the heart of your school identity and practice? How do you communicate this? • Let's borrow the exercise from the Head at Acklam Grange. Write down every school rule from memory. Can you do it? What do you notice?	• How do you know when students are proud of their work? Are there opportunities within your setting to encourage and normalise students being proud of their work? • Are there opportunities within your physical environment to make small amendments to encourage self-regulation? • Do many of your staff choose to send their children to your setting? Do you know why?
Your commitment for further reflection and action 1. 2. 3.	

Harmony Primary School, Belfast

Elaine Johnston, Principal

About us and our community

At Harmony Primary School, the importance of belonging cannot be overstated. Situated in the Glencairn area of North Belfast, our school serves a community with high levels of socioeconomic challenge. A significant proportion of our children are entitled to free school meals, and many of our families experience intergenerational trauma, unemployment, limited access to further education and the daily pressures of social deprivation. For some children, these realities create barriers such as low aspirations, limited access to experiences that build cultural capital, and social, emotional and behavioural needs linked to Adverse Childhood Experiences (ACEs).

I have been privileged to work at Harmony for the past three years, during which time I have seen firsthand how a shared commitment to belonging can transform children's lives and strengthen the entire school and wider community.

What belonging means to us

The emphasis we place on togetherness and unity is captured in our school motto: 'Together we learn, Together we succeed in Harmony.' We are all active in the learning that takes place, strengthened by the successes that we achieve, and responsible for the environment we share – physical and emotional.

Our school values – respect, co-operation, compassion, equality and open-mindedness – are the drivers for turning this vision of belonging into everyday practice at Harmony.

- Respect is demonstrated through restorative conversations that strengthen trust.
- Co-operation is nurtured through group-learning and peer-mentoring.
- Compassion is modelled through how we respond to and support families in crisis.
- Equality is championed through inclusive classrooms where every child is valued.
- Open-mindedness is encouraged through a rich curriculum that broadens horizons.

We are proud to be a community school. We do not see our role as confined to classroom learning. We aim to be a safe harbour where aspirations are nurtured and hope can take root – for our children, their families and our staff.

Agency

Economic hardship and limited access to wider opportunities can put a ceiling on aspiration by inhibiting agency, reducing the extent to which we feel, individually and collectively, that we are able to contribute meaningfully to create change. To counteract this at Harmony, we have a strong emphasis on ensuring that our children's voices are heard, that their contributions matter and that they have real, tangible influence in our school. For us, developing agency is about moving from passive reception to active participation – equipping everyone with the confidence and skills to thrive in school and in society.

In our experience, attending to agency has led to increased confidence and greater engagement in learning, as well as improved attendance among some of our most vulnerable learners – and their families.

Pupil agency

Choice

Within our classrooms and learning environments, we aim to give pupils choice over how they learn.

- **Class charters** are co-created every September, enabling pupils to shape the expectations and responsibilities of their learning environments. Typical examples of pupil-generated statements within class charters include: 'we listen respectfully to one another', 'we try our best and support each other with our learning', 'we make sure everyone feels welcome and included'.
- Children also make choices before key transitions, such as between Nursery and P1 (Primary 1 – the equivalent of Reception in England and Wales), about which work they put in their portfolios for their new teachers, helping them feel control over how they present their learning journey so far.
- Our teachers design lessons that **prioritise choice** by letting pupils make decisions about how they present and record their learning, for example, choices on use of technology or visual media, as well as written work.
- Pupils are responsible for **setting their own goals** and tracking achievement. Using tools such as the New Group Reading Test (NGRT), Accelerated Reader and progress walls, we support them to have meaningful conversations with teachers about their learning. This begins in P1 and runs all the way through to P7, building steadily over time as pupils gain independence. This helps reframe assessment as a shared journey that our children are active in, rather than something that is 'done to them'.
- Our **restorative practice** approach helps children be accountable and responsible for their choices, giving them the skills to repair relationships and reflect on their actions. Instead of sanctions being imposed in isolation, pupils are supported to understand consequences and contribute to solutions.

Leadership

Our pupil leadership roles are not tokenistic; they carry real responsibility. Through opportunities such as School Council, playground buddies, digital leaders and eco-champions, we strive to give children authentic opportunities to represent their peers, lead initiatives and influence decisions. For example, digital leaders are responsible for delivering assemblies on online safety, and School Council members are responsible for developing and communicating our shared Action Plans and Areas of Focus for the year.

Parent agency

We aim to ensure parents feel like active agents in their child's learning and in school life. In a community where many have historically felt disempowered by education, rebuilding trust has been essential.

Family learning workshops

We regularly run family learning workshops to help equip parents with the knowledge and understanding to be active partners in their child's learning. Decisions about what topics we cover are made through parent voice (largely captured through surveys) – in the past this has included literacy, online safety and behaviour strategies.

Educational and social initiatives such as Roots of Empathy (n.d.), and skills-based courses and craft-based clubs (such as 'knit and natter') provide further opportunities for parents and children to learn and grow together. These initiatives are publicly recognised through certificates and local press coverage, validating individual and collective achievement and reinforcing pride in participation.

Two-way communication

We aim for open, two-way dialogue with our parent community, using platforms such as Seesaw, our school website and Facebook, to not only share information but to actively seek feedback and dialogue. Parents are invited to contribute to school improvement discussions and are consulted on curriculum changes and enrichment opportunities.

One example of this type of collaboration was our **Vision and Values Consultation**, where parents played a key role in shaping the direction of the school. The process we followed for this is outlined here.

1. **Parent voice**: We published an online questionnaire in June, inviting parents to share what values they wanted their children to experience at Harmony. The questionnaire included multiple-choice options that had been generated by staff, as well as open-text boxes for parents to make their own suggestions.
2. **Pupil voice**: We explored the same questions with children in class discussions, helping them surface what values were important to them.
3. **Staff reflection**: The whole staff body was involved in reviewing parent and pupil feedback, identifying common themes and language.
4. **Shared decision-making**: A joint working group of key stakeholders including staff, pupils and parents finalised the school's five core values.

The values that were chosen at the end of this process – respect, equality, compassion, co-operation and open-mindedness – were felt by all stakeholders to represent what we as a community needed to instil in our children in order to create a solid foundation for developing lifelong learners and citizens.

One parent had this to share about the process:

> 'I'd never been asked what **I** thought the school's values should be before. When Harmony invited us in for the vision and values workshops, it really meant a lot. We talked about what mattered to our families, and then we actually saw our ideas in the final values. It made me feel like my voice counted – that I wasn't just a parent dropping my child off, but someone who could help shape the school.'

Contributing to our school

We know that our parents can make valuable, meaningful contributions to our school, and we work hard to communicate that to them. Our **community skills and support survey** invites parents to let us know about any skills (whether professional or amateur), contacts or experiences that they would be willing to lend the school. It starts very intentionally with the assumption that our parents **do** have something to share.

As a result, our parents contribute a range of skills to school life: some have supported gardening projects such as planting window boxes around the school, while others contribute their professional expertise via school initiatives such as our careers fair. This helps parents feel that they matter to our community.

Staff agency

It's equally important that our staff feel a sense of agency. We have deliberately fostered a culture of distributed leadership, with middle leaders (including Vice Principal, SENDCo, Curriculum Leads) taking responsibility for driving initiatives and shaping our shared practice.

Collaborative networks

Our participation in the Shankill Principals' Group led to the formation of the first Shankill Primary Area Learning Community, allowing for deeper collaboration across our local area for all levels of leadership. It's important for our staff's ongoing development to have opportunities to learn from others, but it's just as crucial that they get the opportunity to share what they are doing – extending the impact of their practice across the community.

What began as an initial exercise in sharing practice and ideas between school leaders, has grown and diversified into a range of different models and forums for sharing practice.

- Principals from local primary and post-primary schools meet regularly to collectively address issues in our local context.
- Cross-school WhatsApp groups allow staff to access support and advice from colleagues in real time, or to offer support and advice to their peers.
- Curriculum and leadership clusters have been established throughout the Shankill area, providing platforms for middle leaders to share.

One staff member shared:

> 'Being part of the Shankill Area Learning Community has been a game-changer. It's reassuring to know other schools face the same challenges – and we're tackling them together. Sharing practice, moderating work and visiting each other's schools has made me feel part of something bigger than just my own classroom.'

Relations

We all thrive when we are surrounded by people who believe in us, peers who include us and families and communities who walk alongside us. So, the quality of relationships that are cultivated in a school are absolutely crucial for securing the best outcomes (in all senses) for the children we are responsible for educating. Relationships are the threads that hold our school family together, ensuring that no child – or adult – feels alone on their journey.

High expectations with nurture

This is what all staff-pupil relationships are built on at Harmony, and it is reinforced in low-stakes, everyday practice that is consistent across our staff body.

- Teachers greet every child at the door each morning by name, reinforcing that they are seen and valued.

- Classroom assistants provide one-to-one check-ins with vulnerable students, giving space to talk about worries before they have a chance to escalate.
- We know and understand that a child's behaviour is a form of communication and staff are trained to respond with empathy and consistency when things go wrong. Our restorative approach means that conflict is resolved through dialogue and repair, not punishment.

Peer relationships

We recognise that friendships and social connections are critical for belonging, particularly for children who may feel isolated by circumstance, and so we work to actively nurture them.

- Playground buddies help young children settle, promoting kindness and reducing playground incidents.
- Circle time allows children to share feelings, practise empathy and resolve minor conflicts together.
- Cooperative learning strategies are embedded into lessons, encouraging pupils to work collaboratively and value each other's contributions.
- Anti-bullying week is marked by pupil-led assemblies and creative projects that affirm the importance of respect and inclusion.

The home-school relationship

We have invested heavily in strengthening our relationships with parents and families. We want our parents to know that we respect them and understand the challenges they are facing. Many parents and family members in Glencairn experience isolation – cut off from extended family networks, hesitant to engage with services and often uncomfortable communicating with school. We work to remain cognisant of this in all our interactions with families.

Our Family Support Worker (FSW) has been pivotal in helping our parents feel seen and heard at Harmony. Working from our Family Support Hub, they are on hand every day to support parents with whatever they need whether that is a cup of tea and a listening ear or signposting to support services. The FSW works not only to improve vertical relations, between parent and school, but also horizonal relations, between parents.

The impact of having a designated person at Harmony to support our families has been clear.

- Parents who once avoided school events now attend regularly, often encouraged by the FSW's personal invitation and reassurance.
- Families experiencing financial or housing pressures have been signposted to food banks, community grants and advice services - reducing stress on parents and increasing the likelihood that our children are able to show up to school ready to learn.
- The FSW has organised parent support groups - including informal coffee mornings - and established a PTA. Our PTA operates an inclusive model where all parents are automatically members, free to engage at a level that suits them. This structure avoids exclusivity and reminds parents that their presence and contributions are inherently valued, whether minimal or extensive.

Community relationships

We see ourselves not just as a school **in** the community, but a school **of** the community. So the local partnerships we have are very important to us, beyond the local professional networks that we participate in, such as the Shankill Area Learning Community.

We work with local churches, youth services and charities to act responsively and preventively to ease the challenges our families face, particularly those facing barriers such as food poverty, poor mental health and unemployment. It is empowering to collaborate in this way and helps avoid silos by creating a shared holistic approach.

It's also important to us that we are helping our children and families feel pride in their community. Our curriculum topic of 'The Shankill - Where I Belong' links children's learning with local history and identity and is supported by events in our local community.

Space and place

At Harmony we recognise that the physical environments that we inhabit carry powerful messages about inclusion, safety and identity. Our school and the homes of most of our families are located at the end of a long road leading out from the city centre: you would only find yourself here if you were intending to come, it is not 'on the way' to anywhere. There is no doctor's surgery, no dentist, and the nearest large supermarket is at the bottom of a very big hill (and many of our families do not have cars). That physical reality can manifest in feelings of isolation - and, at the extreme, abandonment - in our community. To counteract this at Harmony, we aim to foster a sense of pride, security and ownership, using our school as a space for empowerment.

Classrooms and learning environments

Our classrooms are designed to be inclusive, calm and stimulating. Displays celebrate children's achievement and showcase work from **every** pupil, not only the 'best'. Teachers make use of space to empower pupils with choice. Learning zones within classrooms, as well as outdoor classrooms and Forest School, give children the opportunity to work independently and collaboratively in a range of different environments.

The Family Support Hub

One of the most striking examples of how space shapes belonging at Harmony is our Family Support Hub. We recognised that many parents felt anxious about coming into school to ask for help – often fearing stigma and judgement. We wanted somewhere that parents could go that was on-site but not inside the main school building: somewhere to act as a bridge between school and the community.

Through the generosity of McDonalds, the school was gifted a shipping container, which we repurposed, renovated and turned into our Family Support Hub. Situated at the edge of the car park, it acts as a gateway into our community: a physical symbol of our commitment to meet parents where they are.

The hub's brightly decorated exterior depicts local landmarks and motivational quotations, alongside a signpost that gestures towards the activities and support available within. The space is intentionally open and accessible: its door is never locked, and the entrance is marked by small signals of hospitality such as treats, a small community library and food donations from the local food bank. The hub includes community fridges and freezers stocked with essentials, available without question or stigma. Parents are also welcome to make a hot drink and have a chat – which many choose to do after a particularly difficult drop-off!

As a senior leadership team, we do not monitor or track who visits the hub. This separation ensures confidentiality, reduces stigma, and communicates to families that their dignity is respected.

The impact of this hub has been profound. Parents who once avoided engaging with school now regularly attend events. Families have access to support with everything from establishing bedtime routines to applying for financial support. The hub has become a symbol of trust – a place where parents can belong on their own terms, without fear of exposure. One parent said:

> 'Before the Family Support Hub, I didn't feel comfortable coming into school to ask for help. It felt like everyone would know my business. But having somewhere private to go made a huge difference. I could talk openly, get advice and not feel judged. It helped me get back on my feet – and now I feel part of the school instead of standing on the outside.'

An unplanned impact has also been that the hub acts as a way of keeping us connected to members of our community after they leave the school – whether that be former parents or staff who have retired, many will often pop into the hub to say hello and keep their connection to the school alive.

Lessons we have learned

- **Meet families where they are.** Creating space for parents to show up authentically helps them feel seen and valued, which leads to greater trust and engagement in the school down the line.
- **Values won't be lived if they aren't shared**. It doesn't matter what **your** values are, you won't get buy-in if they aren't aligned with the values of the families and community you serve.
- **Belonging is not a product, it's a practice.** Belonging will never be completed, it is a continual and ongoing process of listening, adjusting and including.

Time to think

Questions for reflecting on your current setting	Questions to consider for further action
• What influence do children and young people have over their learning goals and targets? • Can you identify any disconnections between how you work with parents and how you say you work with parents? • What opportunities do staff have to join local, regional or national networks? Are there opportunities to strengthen local sharing of insights in response to context-specific issues?	• What opportunities (physical and symbolic) are there for you to signal to families that you will meet them where they are? • Do you have parents within your school community who find it difficult to come into school? Are you aware of what barriers are stopping them? What assumptions might be at play? • Do you know what your wider community's values are? How do you know this? How do they compare with your school's values?
Your commitment for further reflection and action 1. 2. 3.	

Time to think: The parent–school relationship

The relationship between school and home is a crucial one. We also know that it can be a challenging one, particularly since the Covid-19 pandemic. Parents, on average, seem to be less supportive of schools (Ofsted, 2023), and there are rising instances of abuse towards school leaders from parents (National Association of Head Teachers, 2023).

When relations between school and families break down, it impacts negatively on the sense of belonging felt by everyone.

- Parents do not feel welcome or listened to.
- Busy school leaders and teachers are placed under greater strain, their efforts perceived as unappreciated.
- And ultimately, children are caught in the middle.

We could spend a lot of time reflecting on how this has happened and who carries the greater share of the blame. If not-belonging is a symptom of how things may have gone wrong, perhaps focusing positively on re-establishing belonging can be a solution. But ultimately it would be more helpful to ask: what can schools and education settings do to improve the quality of relationships they have with parents?

Blueprint for Parent Participation by Parent-Friendly Schools

Since 2020, UK charity Parentkind has engaged with 9500 schools within their network to research best practice in parent participation. Their research has resulted in a Blueprint for Parent Participation (Parentkind, 2020), which you can find on their website.

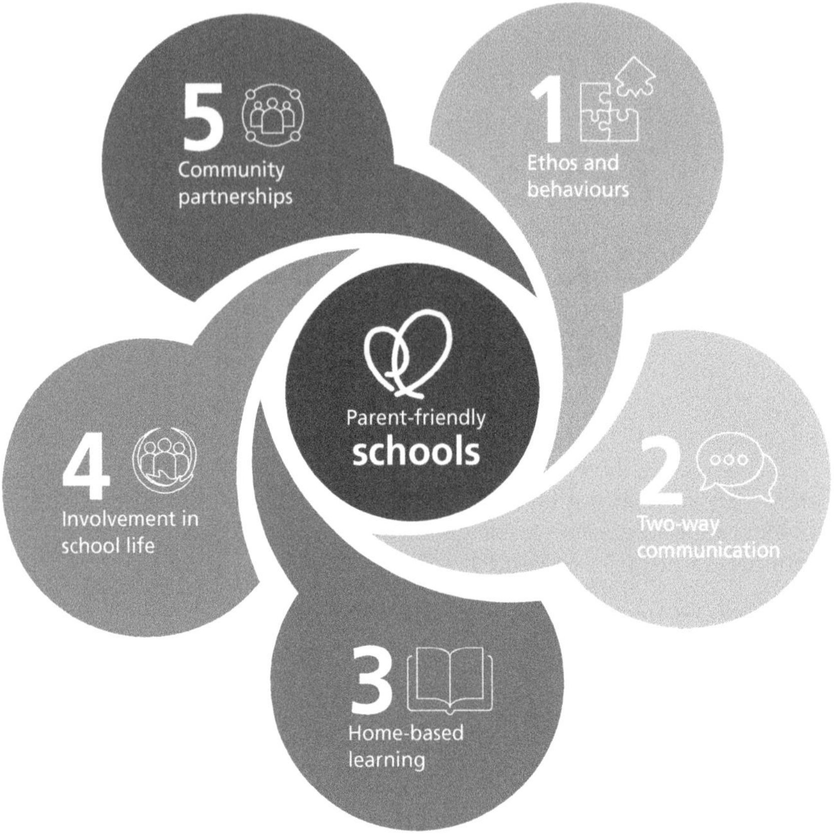

Blueprint for Parent Participation. Reproduced with the permission of Parentkind.

With 5 drivers and 25 initiatives, this framework can support schools in evaluating success and managing onward improvements. It is an evidence-backed way of helping school leaders prioritise and deliver impact.

Questions to consider

We do not have the space here to consider this blueprint in full, but as a starting point we may want to ask ourselves the following.

- How central are parents to our overall strategic plan?
- Do we have a clear and consistent way of working with parents across our staff team?

- Do we consider what parents need from our communication as much as we consider what we want to communicate?
- How are we equipping parents to support effectively with at-home learning?
- How accessible are opportunities for parents to work with us?
- Where are the groups in our local community that parents are actively engaged in? And do we have a relationship with those groups?

Examples in practice

- Both **Harmony Primary School** (page 85) and **Richard Barnes Academy** (page 103) include parents in their reviews of visions and values.
- **Bantock Primary School** (page 29) work with local community groups to understand their needs and priorities better, which has led to their first parent ambassadors.
- **King's Cross Academy** (page 53) think carefully about how they can make at-home learning work better for families.
- **Flakefleet Primary School** (page 17) consider how the parts of the school that are most accessed by parents can be made to feel more welcoming and informal.

Further support

Parent-Friendly Schools offer an accreditation programme (2025) to help schools evaluate their current practice, and PiXL and Parentkind co-published a free resource, *PiXL Insights: Partner with Parents for Impact,* which includes further research, guidance and practice (PiXL and Parentkind, 2025). Both of these are available via the organisations' websites.

Richard Barnes Academy, Peterborough

Sarah Judge, Vice Principal

About us and our community

Richard Barnes Academy (RBA) is part of the Thomas Deacon Education Trust and provides alternative provision for learners who are at risk of, or have experienced, permanent exclusion. Learners' time with us is varied, transient and very much dependent on need.

Our academy operates across two campuses, Trinity and Fitzwilliam. We have 160 commissioned places across the two campuses and welcome learners from all 15 secondary and 61 primary schools across the city of Peterborough.

- Our Trinity campus works with key stages 3 and 4 learners. Our priority at this site is re-engaging our learners, the majority of whom are boys at risk of Child Criminal Exploitation (CCE), with education.
- Our Fitzwilliam campus is mainly home to our primary provision (often learners with high special educational needs) and our GEMs programme, which provides targeted therapeutic and academic support for young people who have been identified as at risk of Child Sexual Exploitation (CSE).

Our cohort is a true reflection of the local context. Peterborough is a city characterised by both rich diversity and areas of significant need. It is a multilingual and multicultural community, home to residents from a wide range of nationalities and linguistic backgrounds. While the city continues to grow and develop, it also faces ongoing social and economic challenges, including relatively high levels of deprivation and unemployment. Peterborough is a very well-connected city, with major transport links including to London. This adds a layer of complexity to our work safeguarding vulnerable young people.

What belonging means to us

The majority of our learners join us following permanent exclusion from mainstream education and so re-shaping their relationship with learning and school is not just important – it's essential. To achieve this, we must first ensure they feel safe and welcomed, and that they are truly being offered a fresh start. Belonging is at the very heart of this.

For many of our learners (and their families and caregivers), the experience of permanent exclusion carries a profound sense of rejection from the very institutions that should nurture and support them, leaving many learners feeling disconnected, unwanted and uncertain about whether education is a space where they can ever succeed.

At Richard Barnes Academy, we recognise that these learners require significant support to rebuild trust, form positive relationships and re-engage with learning. Many have struggled within conventional educational settings and have often faced traumatic experiences. By the very nature of having received a permanent exclusion, most will have encountered at least one Adverse Childhood Experience (ACE), and for many, the exclusion itself becomes an additional layer of trauma.

A strong sense of connection and belonging within our school community acts as a buffer against these negative experiences, replacing feelings of rejection with recognition, acceptance and hope. Through consistent, compassionate interactions and a nurturing environment, we help learners rebuild their self-belief and develop a sense of self-efficacy.

Our core purpose is to support every learner to become the **best version of themselves.** We do this by creating a purposeful, friendly and safe environment rooted in our pillars of **Ambition**, **Character,** and **Safety**. These pillars offer our young people the chance to change the trajectory of their lives, re-engage with education and take ownership of their choices. Our aim is to nurture well-rounded individuals who are equipped to succeed – not just academically, but in all aspects of life.

Space and place

Our **Safe Pillar** is the foundation upon which everything else is built. Before we can talk about ambition or character development, we must ask a simple yet profound question: 'Does this child feel safe?' Safety, for us, means both physical security and psychological safety, where learners feel they belong, their voice matters and they are free from fear of judgement or harm.

Belonging is a fundamental human need. When young people do not find it in positive spaces, they may seek it elsewhere. Unfortunately, our RBA learners are often at risk of being targeted by groups that seek to exploit vulnerability by offering a compelling sense of identity and purpose. To combat this we must make school unmissable – a place where learners feel valued, connected and safe enough to take risks in their learning.

Embedding safety in practice

- **Psychological safety**: Classrooms are spaces where mistakes are part of learning, questions are welcomed and every voice is heard without fear.
- **Trusted relationships**: Every child has an adult who knows them well, notices when something is wrong and acts swiftly to restore security.
- **Visible safeguarding**: Our policies are lived daily – from clear routines to consistent boundaries – showing learners that their wellbeing is our priority.
- **Safe spaces**: Dedicated areas where learners can regulate, reflect and reconnect.
- **Discreet communication**: All staff now wear earpieces connected to their radios, enabling quick, calm responses to incidents without disrupting lessons or alarming learners. This practice supports a stable, focused environment where learning remains the central focus.

Creating a predictable environment

Routines shape our school culture and provide learners with the security they need to thrive. They're not about control – they're about care. They communicate: *You matter. We've thought about your day. We've created a space where you can feel safe, so you can belong and succeed.* Learner voice has been instrumental in shaping these routines, ensuring genuine buy-in from our learners. Together, learners and staff have developed routines that promote positive social norms, establishing consistent expectations, agreed consequences and effective de-escalation processes. These routines are designed for daily application.

To share an example of this in practice, our routine around late arrival to school was adapted directly in response to learner voice.

The original routine

Learners who arrived late were collected five minutes before lunchtime, received their meal early and then ate in a classroom with a member of staff while completing reflection activities linked to the implications of being late.

Learner voice

- Some felt the system unintentionally appeared to reward lateness, as those arriving late accessed lunch before the rest of the school.
- Those receiving the consequence also expressed that they missed the opportunity for a second serving of food – significant for some learners for whom this may be the only substantial meal of the day.
- They highlighted the loss of valuable social time with peers during lunch.

Our reflection

While the original routine could be viewed as a natural and logical consequence intended to deter lateness, we reflected carefully on the broader developmental benefits of shared mealtimes – particularly the social learning that takes place around a table: practising manners, building relationships and learning to conduct oneself appropriately in communal settings.

The new routine

Learners who arrive late now attend lunch at the usual time alongside their peers but sit together at a designated table. After all learners have finished eating, those who were late spend the remainder of the lunch period with a member of staff completing reflection work on the impact of their lateness. This adjustment maintains accountability while preserving access to food and social development opportunities. The changes have been positively received and demonstrate the strength of co-constructed routines built on listening, reflection and shared values.

Why routines matter

For many learners, life outside school is unpredictable. When they enter our doors, they need to know what to expect. Routines also teach our learners responsibility, and over time these habits build independence and prepare them for success both inside and outside the school.

All our routines have clear expectations for both our learners and our staff, emphasising the joint responsibility that we all share. Being explicit about the expectations and responsibility of adults particularly helps to build – and in some cases re-establish – learners' trust in adults.

Routines are prominently displayed in key relevant areas around the campus environment in order to reinforce and remind everyone in our community of their responsibility in upholding then.

Below is an example of one of our routines, and we have deliberately selected one that might be controversial. As part of our welcome routine at RBA, all our young people are wanded: for us, this is an important part of our commitment to safety so that every young person understands their right to feel safe in our school community. Because the purpose behind this is clearly explained when learners are inducted, we have buy-in for this process across our community.

Welcome and wanding

Learners will	Staff will
• Arrive to school on time. • Enter through the front door and greet reception staff. • Hang their coat on a hanger and put personal belongings into their personal folder. • Place folders and bags into their year group box. • Go to a member of staff to be wanded. • Remove their shoes to show they are empty. • Put shoes back on. • Head to the hatch to get breakfast. • Take their breakfast to their tutor room.	• Greet learners as they arrive. • Ensure wallets and the boxes are ready for learners to use. • Respectfully ask learners to turn out their pockets, to raise their arms for wanding, and to take off their shoes. • Use the metal detector wand to check learners, including waistbands. • Check for correct uniform. • Thank learners for cooperating and invite them to collect breakfast from the hatch.

Welcome and wanding routine

Shared spaces

We purposefully build in designated moments within the school day where our whole campus communities come together. For example, at break times and lunch times all learners and staff congregate in a shared area with access to board games, indoor sports equipment (e.g. table tennis tables) and other activities to support interaction and relationship-building. All our learners head to these shared spaces on arrival in the morning and are then accompanied by an adult to their first lessons. This ensures a smooth and purposeful start to every day and therefore contributes to the predictability and consistency experienced by our learners.

Relations

At RBA, relationships are everything. They are at the heart of our work and the foundation of our learners' success. We place a high priority on re-building positive, trusting relationships and this is evident in all staff–learner interactions – from the warm welcome each morning to the time staff spend with learners during breaks and lunchtimes. Once these relationships are established, we can effectively identify and target the support each learner needs – academically, behaviourally and emotionally.

We place equal importance on building strong, collaborative partnerships with parents and carers, as well as with external professionals and colleagues across other city schools. By working together, we create a consistent and supportive network around each learner, ensuring that every aspect of their development and wellbeing is understood, valued and nurtured. Our relational practice ensures that the context of every learner is understood, and their individual needs are met.

Understanding our learners

Any new learner joining RBA undertakes a thorough induction process designed to build a deep understanding of their individual needs. This includes an 'All About Me' activity and GL assessment testing in reading, maths, English, and science, alongside the CAT4 (Cognitive Ability Test) assessment to identify gaps in knowledge and determine the level of support required. Learners also complete the PASS (Pupil Attitudes to Self and School) survey (GL Assessment, n.d.) to capture their current perceptions of school and self. The information gathered is used to determine the most appropriate pathway of provision for each learner and to inform their subsequent timetable. Following testing, a meeting is held with a member of the SLT, the learner and their parent(s) or carer(s) to discuss the outcomes, agree on the support plan and ensure a shared understanding of the next steps. A pupil profile is created for each learner, and where necessary, personalised learning plans are developed to ensure effective access to all lessons.

For our primary learners, they first spend time in their induction class to really get to know them as people, before moving them into the most appropriate permanent teaching class. For our secondary learners, they are allocated a tutor who acts as their advocate.

Parent and carer relations

From the moment learners start with us, we begin building strong relationships with their parents and carers. This starts with the initial induction meeting, where we lay the foundations for open and ongoing communication. From there, we ensure regular home–school contact, with tutors reaching out weekly to share updates and maintain connection. We also hold structured conversations throughout the year that are invaluable for keeping parents informed and engaged (three times a year for secondary learners, and six times a year for primary learners).

We work hard to establish trust and transparency, celebrating achievements and addressing challenges together to secure the best outcomes for each young person. This can be challenging, as many of our families face complex home lives and may be reluctant to engage with education professionals – often due to their own negative experiences of school. That's why we strive to create an environment where parents feel welcome, respected and comfortable attending meetings and events. Where attending in person is a barrier, we will conduct home visits to ensure that home–school liaison remains strong and inclusive. We have invested in a family liaison officer and a family support worker to break down barriers and build supportive relationships with families. Through consistent communication, family meetings and progress reviews, we ensure parents and carers remain fully involved, informed and supported.

External partnerships

We recognise that many of our learners require a holistic network of support that extends beyond the classroom. To achieve this, we work closely with a range of external partners, including Children's Social Care, the Safe Schools Officer and specialist services such as Aspire (a recovery service for drug and alcohol misuse). Due to the correlation between permanent exclusion and undiagnosed SEND, a close partnership with the local authority SEND team is more important than it has ever been.

These partnerships play a crucial role in safeguarding, promoting wellbeing and ensuring that learners feel valued and supported in all aspects of their lives. Regular multi-agency meetings allow us to share information, coordinate interventions and ensure that every learner's voice is heard. By working collaboratively with these partners, we are able to provide consistent messaging, clear boundaries and tailored guidance, helping learners to build trust and stability.

School collaboration

Due to learners frequently transitioning between mainstream settings and RBA, we have aligned our core subject curriculum specifications with those delivered by the majority of local secondary schools, as well as phonics for primary. This ensures continuity for learners moving in and out of the provision, helps mitigate the further formation of gaps in learning and helps learners feel more confident and secure in their learning if/when they move back into mainstream.

We work in close collaboration with the local authority Head of Behaviour and Inclusion and city schools to proactively prevent permanent exclusions by ensuring strategic support is in place for learners at risk. A key part of this approach is guaranteeing our senior leaders' presence on the weekly behaviour panel, where we offer guidance and advice to schools when learners are struggling to engage. Additionally, we provide short-term intervention placements designed to re-set learners, giving them the opportunity to reflect and rebuild routines, with the hope they return to their mainstream setting with renewed focus and support.

Agency

For young people who have had a difficult time in mainstream education, instilling in them the belief that they belong and matter in an educational setting is paramount. Critical to this is creating an environment in which they can be their authentic selves. As mentioned, our core purpose is to support every learner to become the **best version of themselves**. This is central to everything we do, and links strongly to our character and ambition pillars.

'What do you need from Richard Barnes Academy?'

This question was the driver behind recent work across our community and has helped us to redefine our vision and values. We conducted a diagnostic-style audit to gather insights about the school's culture and ethos from staff, learners, parents/carers and a wide range of city-wide stakeholders – including principals, Trust members, Local Authority colleagues and the Safe Schools Police Officer. This process began by bringing everyone together to share their perspectives. This provided real insight and holistic understanding of the needs required from our provision for all involved with it.

Alongside this we reviewed our behaviour policy to ensure it truly reflects our culture, values and strategic direction. Many of our learners have experienced highly punitive behaviour systems in mainstream settings. In contrast, our approach is therapeutic: it helps learners understand the natural consequences of their actions while removing judgement, fostering a sense of ownership over their choices, and promoting self-regulation.

Our therapeutic approach

A therapeutic approach to behaviour doesn't mean getting rid of all rules and boundaries. In fact, a therapeutic approach **relies** on clear, consistent and compassionate boundaries. The difference is in our response when those boundaries are tested. We don't just react; we look for the need behind the behaviour and provide genuine support. It looks to connection before correction. We do not lower expectations; we maintain high standards and ensure consistent follow-up, guiding learners to take responsibility for their actions and achieve their full potential. Poor choices are treated as learning opportunities.

Central to this approach is developing a shared language across the school community for communicating expectations and consequences in a supportive manner, particularly when supporting dysregulated learners or those sensitive to authority. Consistent adult responses reduce confusion, reinforce predictability and maintain a calm, safe environment.

We emphasise choice and natural consequences, empowering learners by helping them recognise how their actions lead to certain outcomes. For example, if a learner is avoiding a lesson, we would say: '**you have the choice** to return to your lesson or continue to avoid it, **but obviously** if you choose to avoid it **the natural consequence** will be that you will have to attend catch-up so that you do not fall behind on your work.' Learners are taught they are accountable for their actions within a safe environment, inviting them to make decisions with a clear understanding of the outcomes.

Promoting positive social norms

It is also important that we reward positive behaviour. Each learner has a **pupil passport,** which they carry to every lesson. Targets are set for the learner, and their progress is **RAG-rated (Red, Amber, Green)** against these targets in each lesson. These ratings are linked to **points**, which act as a currency.

Points can be accumulated and for our secondary learners can be spent in our **school shop**, where learners have the opportunity to purchase both items they need and items they want. Our shop is stocked with an emphasis on self-care items, and also items that learners might like to buy as gifts for family members. Our primary learners also accrue points but instead of spending them on items in the shop they can be used to fund experiences such as soft play, eating out and cinema trips.

This points system motivates learners, reinforces positive behaviours and teaches them about taking responsibility for their choices in a tangible way. Other ways we reward learners include postcards home and positive phone calls, which celebrate success and help learners feel recognised. This is valuable not only for learners but also for their parents and carers, who sometimes also need to see school as a positive and trusting place.

All of these elements collectively cultivate belonging for our learners. Our culture, policies and daily interactions create a community where our learners feel valued, understood, respected, safe and empowered. Perhaps the best evidence of impact comes from those who experience our practice firsthand – our learners:

> 'When I was permanently excluded from my mainstream school, I was expecting to come to Richard Barnes Academy and be treated kind of like a felon. To my surprise though Richard Barnes Academy was the opposite. The staff made me feel like I had been given a second chance, an opportunity to prove that I'm not a "naughty" kid. Although it didn't happen right away I soon warmed up to the idea that we are all in a small community all wanting the same thing – a chance to prove ourselves. Richard Barnes Academy staff and students made me feel like I belonged and reshaped me into the person I am today. For me coming here was the stepping stone I needed to grow as a person. I have been at Richard Barnes Academy for two years now and had the opportunity to go back to mainstream multiple times but I believe Richard Barnes Academy is better suited for me.'

Lessons we have learned

- Belonging begins with the **mindset of the adults**. When we move from 'What's wrong with this learner?' to 'What might have happened to this learner?' we shift from **judgement** to **curiosity**.
- **Empower learner voice** through active listening and ensuring that their voice actually **influences real decisions** – otherwise it is just a token gesture.
- **Work collaboratively** to develop **shared language** to reduce ambiguity and build psychological safety. When staff use different language, apply different expectations or interpret values differently, learners experience uncertainty.

Time to think

Questions for reflecting on your current setting	**Questions to consider for further action**
• Reflect on your transition practices. In what ways are you able to build an accurate picture of a student's relationship with school and learning? How do you uncover what students believe about schools, teachers and themselves? • Do students get a fresh start in your setting? How do you communicate that to them? • Imagine that everything is going to plan for a student – there are no safeguarding or behavioural concerns that mean the school needs to reach out to the parents. In this instance, how often would parents hear personalised feedback about their child and their experience in school?	• Reflect on your rules and the repercussions for breaking the rules. Are there opportunities to strengthen the link between the choices and the natural consequences, to help students understand the impact of their actions? • Do your students and staff have an equal and shared responsibility for contributing to a positive and productive school culture? Is this communicated clearly and transparently? • Are there opportunities to incorporate more student voice into the rituals and routines in your setting?
Your commitment for further reflection and action 1. 2. 3.	

Ferndown Upper School, Dorset

Deneen Kenchington,
Deputy Headteacher

Oli McVeigh, Assistant Headteacher

About us and our community

Located in Dorset on the south coast of England, Ferndown Upper School is a comprehensive co-educational school in an area that is highly selective due to a number of grammar and faith schools nearby. We operate in a three-tier system, so our students join us in Year 9. Due to the highly selective nature of our local area, generally our incoming cohorts of students have lower prior attainment than the local average, but we are proud of the progress our students make with us. Ferndown as an area is very economically diverse: students who live extremely close to one another often come from families in very different income brackets.

Deneen's postgraduate research focused on the critical consciousness of working-class boys. We kept encountering a perception – in research and practice – that there were some teachers who could 'do' boys, and some who could not. We wanted to challenge this and began to carefully consider – supported by a chance encounter with Dr Alex Blower at Arts University Bournemouth (AUB) – whether what we were offering was working for our boys.

This chapter will focus on the work we did with our boys, but the impact of the work has spread across our entire school. Since we began, the attainment gap between boys and girls at Ferndown has closed, but we also have positive progress for our disadvantaged students, and our SEND and IDACI gaps have closed.

What belonging means to us

Here at Ferndown, we believe in developing citizens that can actively engage in their community, and advocate for themselves and others. We know from our research (Deneen's postgrad research, our research in our own school and national research from academics like Dr Blower) that boys often feel they lack connection to their community. We also know that our boys are living in a society that perpetuates harmful messages about masculinity, and that these messages are targeted specifically at boys like ours. We want our boys to understand that there is no single model of positive masculinity, and that they get to choose the type of man they want to be.

Therefore, belonging to us means our boys being truly seen and 'feeling held' by us. We know we have got belonging right when our boys feel able to show up authentically with us.

Our work is underpinned by the ten Taking Boys Seriously (TBS) principles: the result of a longitudinal study by Ulster University which aimed to identify how the adults in boys' lives can support them and help them understand their masculinity (Ulster University, 2021). The TBS principles are focused on understanding boys as relational learners.

1. Recognise the primacy of relationship.
2. Demonstrate dignity and respect.
3. Utilise a 'strengths-based approach' to learning.
4. Challenge and affirm masculine identities.
5. Promote positive mental health.
6. Identify blocks to boys' learning.
7. Connect boys' learning to context.
8. Engage meaningfully with boys.
9. Enable creative learning environments.
10. Value the voice of boys.

At the start of our journey, a small cohort of our boys were involved in the 'Being a Boy' programme at AUB – a flagship, arts-based opportunity for the boys to explore their sense of self and challenge homogeneous stereotypes. We saw from this the lasting impact that adopting this relational approach had on attendance, behaviour and attitude – and this gave us the confidence to author our own programme based on the principles and connecting them to our own specific context.

Our vision is to ensure that our boys have a voice, can articulate their needs – emotional, physical and academic – and are able to reflect on their experiences and values in a safe environment.

Relations

We began to consider the school community from the boys' perspectives: seeking to understand how they saw themselves at school. Because the TBS principles are grounded in understanding boys as relational learners, we began by auditing our context against each of the principles. This built a picture of how and where the boys were being heard, both in our classrooms and through our curriculum. Through this process we were able to identify training needs for staff – around relational practice and the principles themselves – as well as where areas of our wider curriculum and enrichment offer could be adapted, to ensure that we were thinking about our boys holistically.

Staff training

We used educational research, our own experience and the TBS principles to write a framework that provided teachers with much-needed knowledge and, more importantly, strategies to improve their relationships with our boys. These are some of the areas that we have explored together as a staff team.

The Emotional Bank Account

We know that teenagers are going to challenge the adults around them: it's an inevitable part of their development. So we aim to embrace this as part of the reality of working with adolescents – we know that there will be tough messages that need to be delivered and that we will need to enforce boundaries and high expectations. But we need to do that in a way that does not undermine or threaten the relationships that we are building with our young people.

Stephen Covey's metaphor of the Emotional Bank Account (EBA) (Covey, 1989) has helped us think about the level of trust in our relationships with our students. You can make 'deposits' to the shared bank account – positive actions like showing kindness, keeping promises and having integrity. Alternatively, you can make withdrawals – actions that diminish trust, like breaking commitments, interrupting and invalidating the feelings of others.

This helps us keep trust in balance, recognising the shared responsibility of teachers and students in keeping the account in credit. The higher our shared credit with students, the easier it is for us to navigate challenges together when they arise. Conceptualising our relationships in this way has helped us to maintain our high expectations without compromising on our nurture-based approach.

Feeding for fulfilment

We adapted Mark Roberts' strategy of 'feeding for fulfilment' (Roberts, 2022) to ensure that our most disengaged learners had the opportunity to experience success in the classroom. During challenging activities, teachers circulate classes and go to the students who are switched off or stuck, providing them with a verbal scaffold to help them come up with a strong response. When it is time to share as a class, these students are called on to share their answers. Even though the teacher has helped them get there, the positive loop that is instigated when students are able to share a good response helps to build intrinsic motivation.

Purposeful and particular praise

We discussed as a staff team how specific praise can be used to support some of these strategies, but that it had to be genuine and individual in order for the boys to feel that it was meaningful.

We aim for feedback to be specifically related to the choices and actions of the students, while also reinforcing the impact of that choice or action. So in an academic context that might look like: 'I like the way you have really thought carefully about the impact of that word.' And the same applies to personal choices: 'I appreciate the level of kindness that you demonstrated in helping that member of our community.'

Through exploring these and other strategies together, our staff have grown in confidence and foster meaningful educational experiences for our boys, particularly those who previously exhibited signs of disengagement. We have seen more boys being open about areas of weakness, which has led to more bespoke support and in turn improved progress and outcomes. Additionally, they are more willing to have conversations around personal support with external agencies such as counselling services. The greater level of vulnerability that our boys are able to show is testament to their improved sense of belonging.

Trusted adults

Our mentoring programme is a natural extension of this culture of sharing experiences. This is not academic mentoring. It focuses on the lived experience of the students and helps them appreciate their educational journey and feel seen within school.

Mentoring at Ferndown places the boys' voices at the heart of the conversation, and we use the TBS principles to guide mentors through discussion pertaining to memorable learning experiences, barriers to learning and aspiration. This enables boys to reflect in more detail on their learning at school and have open conversations about their context and how this context impacts or enriches their learning goals.

Our mentors are all staff at Ferndown, whether teaching or support staff. Last year, we had around a dozen mentors. Each had been chosen because of the quality of relationships they already had with the students. The minimum requirement was that each mentor would meet with their mentee for weekly sessions over a six-week period. In reality, most met more frequently and retained the contact throughout the academic year.

This programme has been successful in helping boys shape their future and understand how to choose their goals and work towards them. The data we have obtained through this has been vital in developing curriculum hooks for our boys, and for providing opportunities for work experience and other enrichment opportunities. Students can see the fruits of their mentoring reflected all around the school.

Agency

For us, agency is all about our students feeling seen, heard and valued – because only then can they feel as though they are able to make meaningful contributions to our community.

Driven by the voices of boys

Our approach has been student-centred from the start. We initially began working with the small group of boys who participated in the 'Being a Boy' programme at AUB, allowing us to trial some of our ideas and get valuable feedback. Feedback from these initial interventions helped us shape the programme into what it has become, which is curated by the boys.

- The boys **chose their own mentors**, ensuring that they would be paired with a member of staff they felt comfortable with. Initially we had assumed that they would only want to be mentored by male staff, but several of the boys were open to being mentored by female staff.

- **Body image** repeatedly came up as something that our boys were struggling with, particularly in relation to what they were seeing online about 'ideal' male bodies. This led to us taking the boys to a local gym, where they met a trainer who spoke to them about both healthy workout practices and the value of exercise for mental health. We also arranged an external speaker – a former model who had experienced disordered eating as a result of body image pressures – to speak to our boys about his journey and how he protects himself now.
- The boys value experiences that get them outside, requesting that we add both **rowing** and **fishing** activities to the programme.

The 'on-call' process

It was also feedback from our boys that led us to re-consider the on-call process that we had at the time. This process meant that when a student was removed from a lesson, they were not able to rejoin the lesson later. Our boys made it clear that they wanted the opportunity to repair and reintegrate into lessons following a removal.

We piloted a method of allowing restorative practice to take place at the point of removal, providing the student with space to use their voice and feel heard in the moment. We modelled the discourse that we wanted to see between the student and their teacher and provided them with the opportunity to articulate how they were feeling about the situation and the subsequent consequence.

This allowed both staff members and students to feel supported in maintaining the relationship. Staff could allow students to come back into the classroom environment sooner if they wished, and they were given live support during the sanctioning process, allowing them to give the student and the matter their immediate attention without disrupting the flow of the lesson. In this way both staff and students feel a greater sense of agency over resolving issues, and senior leaders are there only to support and facilitate.

High expectations

We believe the notion that boys have low aspiration is a myth – but it is a pernicious one and we work intentionally to combat it through a culture of high expectations. We have built consistency in the way we speak to, and about, our students – especially our boys. Every interaction seeks to communicate that we expect the best from them because we have absolute faith in their ability – and that our school community, and society, needs and values them. We also aim to reinforce the symbiotic nature of teaching and learning: we are here to teach them, and they are here to learn. We are both equally responsible for whether that endeavour is successful.

They won't be able to do it if you don't think they can

This has become a bit of a mantra for us as we seek to raise expectations for all students, especially our boys. We seek to create spaces and provide opportunities for our students to do exceptional things. We set the bar high so that they know we believe they will rise to it, and sometimes to do that we have to stretch them out of their comfort zones.

Bringing it back to the work

When there has been a breakdown in communication or an emotional outburst in a lesson, we try to bring the conversation back to their work. We ask students things such as 'Show me the work you were doing at the time.' or 'What content was being discussed when you began to feel frustrated?' In this way, we're able to acknowledge their feelings, unpick exactly where things started going wrong and redirect the conversation back towards learning.

Being explicit about teacher expertise

A student once said to Deneen, 'What do you know about success, Miss? You never even left school.' The teaching profession is often one of the first professions that children and young people encounter, and because of that it's easy (and perhaps not surprising) for them to assume that there is little impressive or expert about what we do.

So we need to be explicit with our students that we really know what we're talking about. We remind them of the years of experience we have, how many exam cycles we have overseen as departments or as a whole school, where we have examiner experience. If we can say this to a student, it adds a huge amount of weight that we shouldn't underestimate: 'I've been an examiner on this paper for five years. When I tell you that you can get a 7, I am not saying that I **hope** you can get a 7, or that I **think** you can get a 7, I am telling you that I **know** you can.'

Space and place

We began to think of the places in school – physical, cultural, emotional – where we could strengthen boys' sense of belonging in Ferndown.

As is the case in many educational settings, we had significant attainment gaps in English between boys and girls at our school, and there was a pervasive narrative that underpinned this: students felt English was not 'for' boys. English is obviously an incredibly important subject, not only for helping students secure their next steps, but also in terms of ensuring they have the literacy skills to access the rest of the curriculum. We believe that if you are able to win English for the boys, you can win the entirety of their education. We decided to make cultivating a sense of belonging for boys within the English department a strategic priority.

The TBS principles recommend the creation of safe spaces to discuss matters pertaining to masculinity – we know that there is little opportunity for this to take place within the curriculum, but we still felt it was important that our school offered boys the chance to do this. Our work, which began in the English department, has spread across the school and led to additional spaces being created within our school for boys to show up authentically and explore their identity, masculinity and internal worlds.

Cultivating a sense of belonging for boys within the English department

As English specialists ourselves, we were well positioned for this work, and our goal was for boys to feel held within the cultural space of our department.

One barrier that we identified was apathy. We reflected again on our current practice alongside the TBS principles and decided that this apathy could be countered by bringing the boys' voices to the fore (valuing the voices of boys).

We revisited how we were engaging boys in English. We listened to them and adapted our approach based on their feedback.

- We made revision more interactive, accessible and consistent. We used social media platforms such as Instagram to host live Q&A sessions prior to exams. We made sure useful resources were visible within the environments that the boys most commonly accessed.

- We made a promise that nothing they wrote would ever go unmarked: if they were going to make the effort to write an essay, we were going to mark it for them.
- We brought in some external speakers to talk about their relationship with reading, offering different role models to our boys.

These are relatively small things in isolation, but they were impactful because they were done in direct response to what the boys asked of us.

This, alongside the relational approaches, has had a really profound impact, not only on our academic results but also on our boys' relationship with English as a subject and with us as a department. Since we began this work, our disadvantaged boys out-performed the whole cohort in English Language in terms of progress – in fact only our boys with an EHCP did better in terms of progress in English Language. We also narrowed the gender gap in progress in English Literature by +0.25. And the impact has stretched beyond the department: school-wide our disadvantaged boys outperformed our whole cohort in terms of progress.

Co-curated safe spaces

As a consequence of our work in the English department, and across Ferndown, we have been able to create additional spaces for boys to have important conversations with trusted adults both inside and outside the school. We have included two examples here, but it is important to note that these were not pre-planned: they arose organically as the programme developed, as our boys engaged with us and told us what they wanted.

The Boys' Book Club

As part of our programme of external speakers, we brought former rugby player and author Ben Mercer in to speak to our students (Ben now runs an online book club that anyone can engage with remotely on Instagram and TikTok). Ben is a passionate reader and has been able to help our boys consider their place within the world of reading. This has led to an ongoing collaboration between Ben and the school, resulting in a monthly book club based around a short story curriculum (totally separate from our English curriculum). Through a series of books that are engaging and also stretching (including *The Old Man and the* Sea by Ernest Hemingway and *Small Things Like These* by Claire Keegan) they are expanding their reading horizons while also engaging in deep critical and personal conversations.

Theatre troupe

With support from theatre practitioner and educator, Dan Boyden, our Head of Drama has established a Year 9 theatre troupe. We do not offer A-level Drama in our sixth form, and we only had two boys taking GCSE Drama, so we were keen to open up more opportunities for boys to engage with theatre.

Following a workshop that all Year 9 boys attended, students were invited to put themselves forward to audition for the troupe. At the time of writing, there are currently ten boys in the troupe with two more about to audition to join. We were intentional about it being a troupe as opposed to a club: we wanted from the start for it to prioritise togetherness and shared purpose, and for the boys to understand that they would be active participants in the journey.

Over the course of an academic year, the boys are writing and producing their own 20-minute theatre piece, which will be performed at the national Boys' Impact conference in autumn 2026. As part of their creative development, we have taken the boys to see theatre shows such as *Choir of Man* and *Dear England*, as well as on tours of TV and film production studios.

The troupe has christened itself Our Direction which speaks to the level of ownership that the boys feel over their journey and work. The boys regularly elect to stay late on Friday afternoons to work on their show and are extremely dedicated to the project.

Lessons we have learned

- **Value the voice of boys**: They will tell you what they need if they believe that you are really listening.
- **High expectations and a nurture-based approach are not mutually exclusive:** They are two sides of the same coin.
- **Always be willing to challenge assumptions**: We must always be willing to accept that we might not know the best answer and have the courage to question traditional practice.

Time to think

Questions for reflecting on your current setting	Questions to consider for further action
• Reflect on the Taking Boys Seriously (TBS) principles. Where does your school practice align with the principles? Where are your strengths as a school? • Do you know if all your students have access to a trusted adult outside of their family that they can speak to? How do you know? What do you do if you suspect a student does not have access to a trusted adult? • Are there groups of students that may benefit from additional safe spaces in order to explore identity and self-expression?	• Which students (and adults) are the most and least heard in your setting? What opportunities are there to listen with more care to under-represented groups? • How might you be able to identify gaps between teacher perception and teacher action? How could staff be supported to dismantle beliefs that might be limiting their capacity to connect meaningfully with learners? • Ferndown focused specifically on creating a sense of belonging for boys within their English department. Are there areas of the curriculum in your setting where a lack of perceived belonging may be impacting on students' engagement and achievement?
Your commitment for further reflection and action 1. 2. 3.	

Time to think: Moving forward with purpose

I hope that reading this book has provided you with opportunities to both reflect on and affirm your current practice, and inspired potential new avenues to explore in order to strengthen belonging in your setting. In these last few pages we will aim to consolidate what you have been reflecting on and start to shift from thought to action.

What's our story?

The stories that we tell ourselves – about our schools, our communities, ourselves – can be incredibly revealing. In his brilliant book, *Community: The Structure of Belonging* (2008), Peter Block poses these questions that can help us think about the stories we are telling – where they may be helping us and also, crucially, where they may be hindering us.

- 'What is the story about this community or organisation that you hear yourself most often telling? The one that you are wedded to and maybe even take your identity from?
- What are the payoffs you receive for holding on to this story?
- What is your attachment to this story costing you?'

Answering these questions is challenging – we are all deeply wedded to our stories. But it is well worth giving yourself time to reflect on these questions, perhaps with key stakeholders. The answers may very well reveal important implications for belonging in your setting.

Evidencing belonging

It's crucial that we think about the different options available for evidencing belonging. You may already be using some of those listed here, and they are by no means exhaustive. There are benefits and drawbacks to each method, and choosing the right combination of approaches will be necessary to gain an accurate and complete picture.

Quantitative measures

Schools are incredibly data-rich places and you are probably already in possession of lots of quantitative data that can contribute to building a picture of belonging.

- Attendance and behaviour data.
- Engagement in wider enrichment and clubs.
- Parental attendance at parents' evenings and school events.
- Staff retention.

These are obviously not evidence of belonging in and of themselves, but they can provide useful jumping-off points for further exploration.

There are also a wide range of measurement tools available. Education and developmental psychologist Kelly-Ann Allen has curated an incredibly helpful library of these on her website (Allen, n.d.).

You may also want to consider tools such as *The Good Childhood Index* (The Children's Society, n.d.) or the Stirling Children's Well-being Scale (Liddle and Carter, 2015). There are also many organisations that support settings in surveying pupil, teacher and parent populations.

Qualitative measures

Although quantitative measures can help expose trends in belonging, or highlight areas that require further exploration, it is often helpful to turn to qualitative measures in order to gain deeper insights.

Gathering authentic voice – for students, staff, parents – is of course central to this. Reflect on current practice for gathering voice. What does it tell you? Who do you hear from the most – and the least? There may be groups of pupils, staff or parents that you need to listen to particularly carefully. Are the ways that you are gathering that voice accessible to everyone you need to hear from? Are you being clear about **why** you are asking for feedback?

For some groups, we may want to consider deep, focused listening projects that provide space to really explore issues relating to identity, belonging and school. Creative arts-based projects such as *Being a Boy* by Arts University Bournemouth (Arts University Bournemouth, n.d.) and *Pull Up a Chair* by the University of Sunderland (Pull up a Chair Project, n.d.) are just two examples of how creating space for young people to genuinely and freely express themselves can be transformational.

The Mattering Matrix

We have seen how a sense of agency – feeling as though we are able to contribute positively within a community – is crucial to building belonging. Psychologist Isaac Prilleltensky states that there are two fundamental human drives that underpin this: the need to feel valued and the need to add value (Prilleltensky and Prilleltensky, 2021). Rachel Johnson has adapted this work into a simple, but powerful, quadrant called the Mattering Matrix (Johnson, 2026).

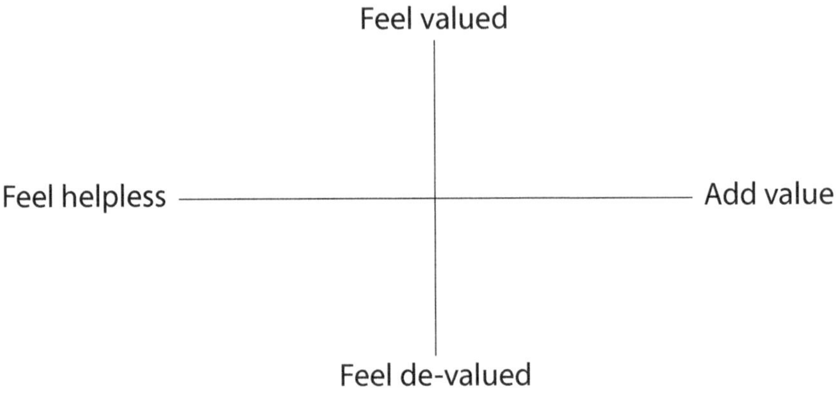

The Mattering Matrix

We can use the intelligence that we gather from quantitative and qualitative measures alongside this matrix to identify who in our communities is at risk of feeling de-valued, or feeling that they do not add value.

Lag measures and lead measures

In *The 4 Disciplines of Execution* by Chris McChesney, Sean Covey and Jim Hulling, they explore the importance of using both **lag** and **lead** measures (McChesney, Covey and Huling, 2012).

All of the measures that we have explored already are **lag** measures. They are results-oriented and backward-looking. They tell us about the effectiveness of what has been done in the past. That's useful. But it doesn't help us think about present and future actions.

Lead measures, on the other hand, are predictive, forward-looking and based on action. They are based on what you can do now that you believe will bring about the desired result, even if the data that shows the impact lags behind.

So, if we are wanting to improve the quality of the relationship with a particular parent, a lag measure might be that there is greater engagement from that parent over time, as evidenced through attendance at parents' evenings, school events and through a warmer tone in interactions. But a lead measure might be that the form tutor makes a point of calling home every two weeks with positive news about how their child is getting on in school.

Or, similar to the approaches taken by **King's Cross Academy** (page 49) and **Acklam Grange School** (page 78), lead measures might be about ensuring that there are regular, timetabled opportunities to discuss every single child in the school at SLT level across the year.

Keeping hold of our agency

The great thing about lead measures is that they affirm and strengthen our own sense of agency. The education sector is challenging to work in, and there are many ways that we operate that can diminish our own sense of professional agency. It's vitally important that we try to retain this, for ourselves and for the children and communities that we serve.

Over the course of writing this book, I have read a lot, visited a lot of schools and had many hours of conversations with school leaders and stakeholders about belonging. If I have one top-level observation from this process, it is that all of the leaders who appear in this book have a strong sense of agency: they build out from the strengths in their practice, they are curious and attuned to where new opportunities may present themselves and, perhaps most importantly, **they believe that they can and will make a positive difference**.

At PiXL we are passionate believers in the power of networking and sharing practice across institutions for building agency within our leadership. So consider this our open invitation to you: if you are doing something that you are proud of, something that you think is working, or if you have learned some lessons that you think others in the profession would benefit from hearing – **please share it**.

This book is the beginning of what we hope will be an ongoing and evolving national conversation about belonging in schools. We would love for you to be part of that conversation – we know you have something of value to contribute.

References

Allen, K-A. (2020) *The psychology of belonging*. Routledge.

Allen, K-A. (n.d.). *Measurement tools*. Available at: https://www.drkellyallen.com/measurement-tools (Accessed: 12 March 2026).

Arts University Bournemouth. (n.d.) *Being a boy: Student opportunities*. Available at: https://aub.ac.uk/schools-hub/widening-access-to-aub/being-a-boy-student-opportunities (Accessed: 12 March 2026).

Banks, V. and Garforth, L. (2022) *PROCLAIM: Providing Rich Opportunities for Children who are Looked After in Middlesbrough*. Middlesbrough Council. Available at: https://moderngov.middlesbrough.gov.uk/documents/s15048/proclaim%20breifing%20paper.pdf (Accessed: 26 June 2026).

Battistich, V. and Hom, A. (1997). 'The relationship between students' sense of their school as a community and their involvement in problem behaviors', *American Journal of Public Health*, 87(2), 1997–2001. Available at: https://ajph.aphapublications.org/doi/abs/10.2105/AJPH.87.12.1997 (Accessed: 12 March 2026).

Block, P. (2008). *Community: The structure of belonging*. Berret-Koehler Publishers.

Bronfenbrenner, U. (1979). The ecology of human development: Experiments by nature and design. Harvard University Press.

Cohen, G.L. (2022). Belonging: The science of creating connection and bridging divides. Norton.

Covey, S.R. (1989). *The 7 habits of highly effective people*. Simon & Schuster.

Department for Education. (2025). *Overview of the Turing Scheme, 2025 to 2026*. Available at: https://www.gov.uk/government/publications/turing-scheme-international-placements-2025-to-2026/overview-of-the-turing-scheme-2025-to-2026 (Accessed: 12 March 2026).

Dix, P. (2017) *When the Adults Change, Everything Changes: Seismic Shifts in School Behaviour*. Independent Thinking Press.

Epley, N. (2014). Mindwise: Why we misunderstand what others think, believe, feel and want. Vintage.

GL Assessment. (n.d.) *Pupil attitudes to self and school (PASS) survey*. Available at: https://www.gl-assessment.co.uk/products/pupil-attitudes-to-self-and-school-pass/ (Accessed: 12 March 2026).

Goodenow, C. and Grady, K.E. (1993). 'The relationship of school belonging and friends' values to academic motivation among urban adolescent students', *The Journal of Experimental Education*, 62(1), 60–71. Available at: https://www.jstor.org/stable/20152398 (Accessed: 12 March 2026).

Grant, A. (2021). Think again: The power of knowing what you don't know. Ebury.

Greany, T., Pennacchia, J., Graham, J. and Bernardes, E. (2023). *Belonging schools: How do relatively more inclusive secondary schools approach and practise inclusion?* Teach First. Available at: https://www.teachfirst.org.uk/sites/default/files/2024-09/3516%20Belonging%20Schools%20Report%20Update.pdf (Accessed: 11 March 2026).

Guidara, W. (2022). Unreasonable hospitality: the remarkable power of giving people more than they expect. Ebury Edge.

Harrison, M.E. *et al.* (2015). 'Systematic review of the effects of family meal frequency on psychosocial outcomes in youth', *Canadian Family Physician,* 61(2), e96–e106.

Haun, D.B., and Tomasello, M. (2011). 'Conformity to peer pressure in preschool children', *Child Development,* 82 (6), 1759–1767. Available at: https://onlinelibrary.wiley.com/doi/abs/10.1111/j.1467-8624.2011.01666.x (Accessed: 12 March 2026).

ImpactEd Group. (2025). *Mind the engagement gap: A national study of pupil engagement in England's schools.* Available at: https://www.impactedgroup.uk/research-campaigns-and-resources/mind-the-engagement-gap-a-national-study-of-pupil-engagement-in-englands-schools (Accessed: 12 March 2026).

Johnson, R. (2026). *Common problem, impactful solution.* PiXL Secondary National Conference, 30 January, London.

Kross, E. (2021). Chatter: The voice in our head and how to harness it. Vermilion.

LAMDA (n.d.) *Our Exams*. LAMDA. Available at: https://www.lamda.ac.uk/lamda-exams/our-exams (Accessed: 24 June 2026)

Liddle, I. and Carter, G.F.A. (2015). 'Emotional and psychological well-being in children: the development and validation of the Stirling Children's Well-being Scale', *Educational Psychology in Practice*, 31(2), 174–185.

Matters, G., Luke, A., Barrett, R. and Land, R. (2004). *The new basics research report.* Available at: http://wayback.archive.org/web/20110330001654/http://education.qld.gov.au/corporate/newbasics/docs/nbftech.doc (Accessed: 30 January 2026).

McChesney, C., Covey, S. and Huling, J. (2012). The 4 disciplines of execution: Achieving your wildly important goals. Simon and Schuster.

Miller, D.P. *et al.* (2012). 'Family meals and child academic and behavioral outcomes', *Child Development*, 83(6), 2104–2120.

National Association of Head Teachers. (2023). *Abuse towards school staff must stop, says NAHT*. Available at: https://www.naht.org.uk/News/Latest-comments/Press-room/ArtMID/558/ArticleID/2653/Abuse-towards-school-staff-must-stop-says-NAHT (Accessed: 12 March 2026).

Ofsted. (2023). *Ofsted annual report 2022/23: Education, children's services and skills.* Ofsted. Available at: https://www.gov.uk/government/publications/ofsted-annual-report-202223-education-childrens-services-and-skills (Accessed: 12 March).

Osterman, K.F. (2000). 'Students' need for belonging in the school community', *Review of Educational Research*, 70(3), 323–367. Available at: https://journals.sagepub.com/doi/10.3102/00346543070003323 (Accessed: 12 March 2026).

Over, H. (2016). 'The origins of belonging: social motivation in infants and young children', *Philosophical Transactions of the Royal Society B: Biological Sciences*, 371(1686), 20150072. Available at: https://royalsocietypublishing.org/rstb/article/371/1686/20150072/22753/The-origins-of-belonging-social-motivation-in (Accessed: 12 March 2026).

Parent-Friendly Schools. (2025). *Accreditation services.* Available at: https://www.parentfriendlyschools.org/p/accreditation (Accessed: 11 May 2026).

Parentkind. (2020). *Blueprint for parent-friendly schools.* Available at: https://www.parentkind.org.uk/assets/resources/Blueprint-for-Parent-Friendly-Schools.pdf (Accessed: 26 March 2026).

PiXL and Parentkind. (2025). *PiXL insights: Partner with parents for impact.* PiXL. Available at: https://www.pixl.org.uk/attachments/download.asp?file=10&type=pdf (Accessed: 12 March 2026).

Prilleltensky, I. and Prilleltensky, O. (2021). How people matter: Why it affects health, happiness, love, work, and society. Cambridge University Press.

Pull up a Chair Project. (n.d.). *The pull up a chair films.* Available at: https://livingarchive.net/view/0064770570825897248 (Accessed: 1 March 2026).

Rethinking Assessment. (2026). *Rethinking Assessment.* Available at: https://rethinkingassessment.com/ (Accessed: 12 March 2026).

Riley, K., Coates, M. and Allen, T. (2020). *Belonging, behaviour and inclusion in schools: What does research tell us? Literature review.* National Education Union. Available at: https://neu.org.uk/sites/default/files/2023-04/Belonging%20research%20Literature%20Review.pdf (Accessed: 11 March 2026).

Riley, K., Coates, M. and Perez Martinez, S. (2018). *Place and belonging in schools: Unlocking possibilities.* The Art of Possibilities. Available at: https://www.theartofpossibilities.org.uk/docs/PlaceAndBelongingUnlockingPossibilities_28_03_2018.pdf (Accessed: 12 March 2026).

Roberts, M. (2022). The boy question: How to teach boys to succeed in school. Routledge.

Robinson, S., Culbert, C. and Smith, P.K. (2025). *Final report for baseline data for the Belonging Matters pilot programme.* National Children's Bureau. Available at: https://www.ncb.org.uk/sites/default/files/uploads/files/Final%20BM%20Report.pdf (Accessed: 11 March 2026).

Roots of Empathy (n.d.) *Roots of Empathy.* Available at: https://uk.rootsofempathy.org/ (Accessed: 12 March 2026).

The Children's Society. (n.d.) *The good childhood index.* Available at: https://www.childrenssociety.org.uk/information/professionals/good-childhood-index (Accessed: 12 March 2026).

Ulster University. (2021). *Taking boys seriously: Boys as relational learners – principles*. Ulster University. Available at: https://www.ulster.ac.uk/__data/assets/pdf_file/0016/1511242/UU-TBS-Principles.pdf (Accessed: 12 March 2026).

Utter, J., *et al.* (2018). 'Family meals among parents: Associations with nutritional, social and emotional wellbeing', *Preventive Medicine*, 113, 7–12.

Vygotsky, L.S. (1978). Mind in society: The development of higher psychological processes. Harvard University Press.

Walton, G.M. and Cohen, G.L. (2011). 'A brief social-belonging intervention improves academic and health outcomes of minority students', *Science*, 331(6023), 1447–1451. Available at: https://www.science.org/doi/10.1126/science.1198364 (Accessed: 12 March 2026).